Countervailing Forces in Afric
Activism, 1973–

In a first-ever longitudinal study assessing black civic participation after the civil rights movement, Fredrick C. Harris, Valeria Sinclair-Chapman, and Brian D. McKenzie demonstrate that the changes in black activism since the civil rights movement are characterized by a tug-of-war between black political power on one side and economic conditions in black communities on the other. As blacks gain greater access and influence within the political system, black participation in political activities increases while downward turns in the economic conditions of black communities produce less civic involvement in black communities. During the course of black activism from the early 1970s to the 1990s, the quest for black political empowerment and the realities of economic and social life acted as countervailing forces in which negative economic and social conditions in black communities weakened the ability of blacks to organize so that their political voices could be heard.

Fredrick C. Harris is Associate Professor and Director of the Center for the Study of African-American Politics at the University of Rochester. Previously he was a visiting scholar at the Russell Sage Foundation and was named a Fellow at the Woodrow Wilson International Center for Scholars. Harris is the author of *Something Within: Religion in African-American Political Activism*, which won the V.O. Key Award for Best Book in Southern Politics, the Distinguished Book Award from the Society for the Scientific Study of Religion, the Best Book Award from the National Conference of Black Political Scientists, and the Choice Award.

Valeria Sinclair-Chapman is Assistant Professor of Political Science at the University of Rochester. She is coauthor with William D. Anderson and Janet M. Box-Steffensmeier of "The Keys to Legislative Success in the U.S. House of Representatives," *Legislative Studies Quarterly* (2003). Sinclair-Chapman's research examines the substantive and symbolic representation of black interests in Congress as well as minority agenda-setting on the national level.

Brian D. McKenzie is Assistant Professor of Political Science at Texas A&M University. Prior to joining the Texas A&M University faculty he was a visiting assistant professor at Emory University. He was also a Fellow at the University of Rochester Center for the Study of African-American Politics from 2002 to 2003. His work has appeared in *Political Research Quarterly*, *Journal for the Scientific Study of Religion*, and *African-American Research Perspectives*.

Countervailing Forces in African-American Civic Activism, 1973–1994

FREDRICK C. HARRIS
University of Rochester

VALERIA SINCLAIR-CHAPMAN
University of Rochester

BRIAN D. McKENZIE
Texas A&M University

CAMBRIDGE
UNIVERSITY PRESS

CAMBRIDGE UNIVERSITY PRESS
Cambridge, New York, Melbourne, Madrid, Cape Town, Singapore, São Paulo

Cambridge University Press
40 West 20th Street, New York, NY 10011-4211, USA

www.cambridge.org
Information on this title: www.cambridge.org/9780521849364

First published 2006

Printed in the United States of America

A catalog record for this publication is available from the British Library.

Library of Congress Cataloging in Publication Data

Harris, Fredrick C., 1962–
Countervailing forces in African-American civic activism, 1973–1994 /
Fredrick C. Harris, Valeria Sinclair-Chapman, Brian D. McKenzie.
p. cm.
Includes bibliographical references and index.
ISBN 0-521-84936-5 (hardback) – ISBN 0-521-61413-9 (pbk.)
1. Political participation – United States. 2. African Americans – Politics and government. 3. African Americans – Economic conditions. 4. African Americans – Social conditions. I. Sinclair-Chapman, Valeria, 1969–. II. McKenzie, Brian D., 1971–. III. Title.
JK1924.H37 2005
323.1196′073′009′045–dc22 2005004573

ISBN-13 978-0-521-84936-4 hardback
ISBN-10 0-521-84936-5 hardback

ISBN-13 978-0-521-61413-9 paperback
ISBN-10 0-521-61413-9 paperback

To the political activists who made a difference despite the odds:
Ella Baker, Fannie Lou Hammer, and Bayard Rustin

And to the political scientists on whose shoulders we stand:
William E. Nelson, Jr., Hanes Walton, Jr.,
and Linda Faye Williams

Contents

Figures and Tables

FIGURES

TABLES

Acknowledgments

In writing this book, we are indebted to a number of people and institutions. We are especially grateful to the administrators at the University of Rochester who provided financial and intellectual support for our research. In particular, we thank the Dean of Faculty, Thomas LeBlanc, for his consistent financial support of the Center for the Study of African-American Politics. Through its postdoctoral fellowship and other resources, the center provided an intellectually stimulating space for us to exchange ideas and flesh out our research approach.

We appreciate numerous colleagues for their helpful discussions and comments as we worked through several versions of this manuscript, including Janet Box-Steffensmeier, Robert Brown, Kevin Clarke, Darren Davis, Richard Niemi, Lester Spence, and Katherine Tate. We also benefited from discussions arising from presentations at the National Conference of Black Political Scientists and the Southern Political Science Association meetings and from workshops including the Conference on Minority Political Participation held at Rutgers University, among others.

We thank our colleagues in the Departments of Political Science at the University of Rochester and Texas A&M University for their support. Each of us is grateful to be working in departments alongside some of the best minds in the discipline. We are especially grateful to Texas A&M University for providing Brian McKenzie with research time to dedicate to this project; to the Ford Foundation for postdoctoral research support for Valeria Sinclair-Chapman; and, to the Russell Sage

Foundation for supporting Fredrick Harris during the early conceptual stages of this project.

We thank the University of Rochester Department of Political Science for providing Lanni Fellowships to fund several of our research assistants during the years we worked on this project. The W. Allen Wallis Institute of Political Economy also provided funds for research assistance. The quality research assistance we received from current and former graduate students at the University of Rochester was indispensable. For their work during various stages of research, we owe D. Vincent Fitts, Anthony Perkins, Aaron Wicks, and especially Robert Walker a debt of thanks. Thoughtful comments from graduate students Lorrie Frasure (of the University of Maryland) and Matthew Platt were also appreciated as we proceeded.

We also thank Blackwell Publishing for allowing us to reprint material from our article "Macro-Dynamics of Black Political Participation in the Post-Civil Rights Era" in the *Journal of Politics* and the Chevron-Texaco Corporation for giving us permission to reprint the Gulf Oil trademark in the advertising ad "We the People . . . How to make the 'political machine' work for you." We would also like to thank Warner Brothers Publishing for giving us permission to reprint the lyrics, "Ain't No Stopping Us Now": Words and music by Allen Cohen, Gene McFadden, and John Whitehead, © 1978 Warner-Tamerlane Publishing Corp., All Rights Reserved, Used by Permission, WARNER BROS. PUBLICATIONS, U.S. INC., Miami, FL 33014.

1

Introduction

> To be a poor man in a land of dollars is hard, but to be a poor race in a land of dollars is the very bottom of hardships.
>
> W. E. B. DuBois, *Souls of Black Folk*, 1903

> Black power recognizes – it must recognize – the ethnic basis of American politics as well as the power-oriented nature of American politics. Black power therefore calls for black people to consolidate behind their own, so they can bargain from a position of strength.
>
> Stokely Carmichael and Charles V. Hamilton, *Black Power*, 1967

The words of W. E. B. DuBois and those of Stokely Carmichael and Charles Hamilton a half century later represent a quandary for African Americans in their quest for political equality in America. By the turn of the century when DuBois wrote that to be a "poor race in the land of dollars is the very bottom of hardships," the political gains that African Americans had received in the aftermath of the Civil War had vanished. Confined to the land that had held them in bondage during slavery with the backing of vigilante violence and the legal complicity of the federal and southern state governments to boot, most African Americans struggled in a state of semiservitude for more than a half a century. Even though DuBois debated Booker T. Washington over the need to restore blacks' citizenship rights, favoring the fight for political rights over Washington's strategy of blacks building a firm economic foundation to prove themselves citizens before the white world, DuBois, as this quote suggests and as he would realize decades later, recognized blacks' political limitations in a society that marginalized blacks as both citizens and workers.

Writing after the legal triumphs of the landmark civil rights legislation that barred racial discrimination and restored blacks' voting rights during the nation's "Second Reconstruction," civil rights activist Stokely Carmichael and political scientist Charles Hamilton argued in their book, *Black Power*, for the need of blacks to gain political influence through mainstream politics. Indeed, the civil rights movement and the legal protections of the 1965 Voting Rights Act (VRA) created new possibilities for black inclusion in local and national politics. These changes in American life opened political opportunities for blacks that facilitated the transition from protest activism to mainstream politics. As Frances Fox Piven and Richard Cloward describe the decline of the civil rights movement and the transition to insider politics: "[I]n virtually no time at all the movement had been incorporated into the electoral system, its leaders running for office throughout the South and its constituencies enjoined to devote their energies to making these bids for office a success in the name of 'black power' " (1979, 253). Like DuBois, Carmichael later recognized the limitations of reforming racial inequality through the political system and advocated the radical transformation of the nation's political and economic system (Carmichael and Thelwell 2003). Hamilton would decades later chronicle the barriers facing civil rights organizations in their efforts to address the economic needs of African Americans in an era when black incorporation into mainstream political life had been firmly secured (Hamilton and Hamilton 1997).

This book considers the state of black political equality in the post–civil rights era by exploring how economic and political forces in American life affect black civic participation. We see the quest for black political empowerment and the realities of social and economic distress in black communities as two sets of competing, and often conflicting, forces on black civic life that simultaneously provide barriers to and opportunities for black civic activism. Our approach to understanding the dynamics of black civic participation in the post–civil rights era is important on several dimensions. As many scholars of civic life in America have argued, participation allows the voices of citizens and organized interests to be heard in the political system. Sidney Verba, Kay Lehman Schlozman, and Henry Brady note, for instance, that civic activism is "not only about individuals – what they do and why they do it," because, "more than in most democracies voluntary activity in America shapes the allocation of economic, social, and cultural benefits and contributes to the achievement of collective purposes" (1995, 7). Expanding political opportunities in the aftermath of the modern civil rights movement provided African Americans with a means to have their voices heard inside rather than outside the domains of American mainstream political life.

But what if the capacity to have voices heard in the political system is stifled by economic and social circumstances beyond the control of individuals or organized interests? This is a question we pose as we consider the civic activism of African Americans in the post–civil rights era, a period during which African Americans experienced unprecedented gains in the political system and also remained at the social and economic margins of American life. As we show in this study, the dynamics of black civic activism in the post–civil rights era is characterized by a tug-of-war between black political empowerment on one side and economic and social distress in black communities on the other. As blacks gain greater access and influence within the political system, the competitive forces of empowerment tug favorably toward increasing levels of black activism while downward spirals in the economic and social conditions of black communities pull toward less civic engagement. As our study chronicles, this tug-of-war demonstrates that the quest for black empowerment and the realities of economic and social life act as countervailing forces in African-American civic life, where persistently detrimental economic and social conditions in black communities weaken the capacity of blacks to have their voices heard as civic actors.

BLACK EMPOWERMENT AND BLACK CIVIC ACTIVISM

One of the questions often asked about the political progress of African Americans in the post–civil rights era is "to what extent has black social and political participation changed since the 1960s?" Just as the civil rights movement declined in late 1960s, the process of blacks' inclusion into mainstream American politics began its ascendancy. This process of inclusion has been described variously in the political science literature as political empowerment and political incorporation, and for this study, we use the concepts interchangeably (Tate 1994; Smith 1996; Leighly 2001; Tate 2004). Urban politics scholars use the concept of incorporation to examine how effectively the interests of minority groups are represented in policy-making (Browning, Marshall, and Tabb 1984; Stone 1989). In their study of the influence of African Americans and Latinos in city politics, Rufus Browning, Dale Rogers Marshall, and David Tabb measure incorporation by the number of minorities on city councils, whether minorities are a part of the city's governing coalition, and whether there is minority control of the mayor's office (1984, 25). In their study of black social and political participation, Lawrence Bobo and Franklin Gilliam, define black empowerment, a term they see as interchangeable with black incorporation, as "increases in the control of institutionalized power" in which blacks have "achieved significant representation and influence in political decision-making" through their control of the mayor's office (1990, 377–78).

Our view of black empowerment and incorporation is twofold and differs somewhat from perspectives in the urban politics literature. First, we are interested in the instrumental value that descriptive representation and greater access to the political system bring to black civic activism rather than incorporation as a feature of decision-making in representative institutions. For the purposes of our analysis, we view political access and representation as signals to civic actors in black communities to engage in mainstream politics. As Bobo and Gilliam argue in their study, when "blacks hold more positions of authority, wield political power, and have done so for longer periods of time, greater number of blacks should see value in sociopolitical involvement" (1990, 379). Second, our conceptualization of incorporation derives from the literature on social movements and black politics (Piven and Cloward 1979; Tate 1994; Smith 1996; Tate 2004). We are interested in the participatory consequences of the incorporation of the civil rights movement into mainstream politics where blacks shifted their energies away from marching in the streets and boycotting businesses and turned to insider modes of civic activity such as contacting public officials about problems and working to get political candidates elected.

While protest activism continued to characterize some aspects of black political life in the post–civil rights era, the movement shifted away from protest as a political strategy to the sphere of electoral politics (see Figure 1.1). As southern blacks began to exercise their political muscle in the aftermath of the passage of the 1965 Voting Rights Act, engagement in mainstream politics became the dominant mode of black civic participation. The VRA "substantially changed the structure of black politics, giving Black Americans new access to the dominant forums within institutionalized politics" (Tate 1994, 16). This process of incorporation was symbolized by the "new black politics" scholarship, which chronicled African-American involvement in mainstream forms of political activities (Shingles 1981; Walton 1985; Morrison 1987; Bobo and Gilliam 1990; Tate 1991; Tate 1994; Tate 2004).

Civil rights strategist Bayard Rustin (1971) suggested, as early as 1964, that if blacks were going to affect politics, they would have to move away from protest and become a part of the political mainstream in American life. "A conscious bid for political power is being made, and in the course of that effort a tactical shift is being affected," Rustin observed. "Direct-action techniques are being subordinated to a strategy calling for the building of community institutions or power bases.... What began as a protest movement is being challenged to translate itself into a political movement" (1971, 112). In the post–civil rights era, Rustin's call for a new strategy has been largely answered as blacks have secured a place in the mainstream of American political life (Browning et al. 1984; Smith 1996; Reed 1999; Gomes and Williams 1992).

At the turn of the twenty-first century blacks have achieved what was unthinkable in the early twentieth century. The number of blacks elected to public office in the nation has skyrocketed. Over forty members of Congress are black, providing members of the Congressional Black Caucus a bloc of votes that can influence legislative outcomes (Bositis 1994; Singh 1998; Canon 1999). Hundreds of blacks have been elected to state legislatures and thousands more have been elected to other state and local offices. These trends in black office-holding and party activism confirm the incorporation of the civil rights movement into mainstream politics. As Robert Smith explains the process of incorporation, "a group previously excluded from the systematic institutions and processes is brought into these institutions and processes, either because it poses a threat to system stability or maintenance or because it is part of the normal, evolutionary adjustments of a

FIGURE 1.1. "We The People . . . How to make the 'political machine' work for you." Source: *Crisis*, June/July 1977

democratic society to claims of new groups for inclusion, incorporation, or integration" (1996, 21). Evidenced by examples such as the contentious seating of the Mississippi Freedom Democratic Party at the 1964 Democratic Convention, as well as the more recent prominent roles of black political actors and organizations such as Jesse Jackson, Condoleezza Rice, and the Congressional Black Caucus, black incorporation has been the result of both the threat reduction and evolutionary adjustments Smith describes.

The rise of black political empowerment is believed to be one of the primary factors that stimulated black civic participation since the civil rights movement. In the immediate aftermath of the passage of the 1965 Voting Rights Act, black office-seeking and black office-holding not only stimulated voter registration and turnout in black communities, but it also fostered civic activities in black communities beyond the voting booth. Those effects were immediately realized in the South, where blacks flexed their political muscle and converted the energy generated from protest campaigns into electorally directed activism. As James Button notes in his analysis of the civil rights movement's impact on social and political change in the South:

> Besides working on the inside to improve conditions, black elected officials were frequently instrumental in promoting increased political participation by black citizens. Not only were blacks much more likely to register and vote when a member of their race competed for public office, but in numerous other ways minority citizens were more attentive to and involved in local politics when a black assumed office. (1989, 227)

Indeed, the participatory effects of emerging black empowerment, especially in the South, were observed by black officeholders themselves. These newly elected officials often attributed their success to a black electorate that contributed to their campaigns in a variety of ways. As these officials reported during the 1960s and early 1970s, their black constituents became active in their campaigns by contributing money, by canvassing voters on their behalf, and by becoming generally more attentive to politics and governance in their communities. For instance, Barbara Jordan, who would later become one of the first blacks to be elected to Congress from the South after Reconstruction, noted how her election to the Texas State House in 1966 stimulated the political participation of blacks in her district. She observed a "new awareness of politics on the state level among Negro voters in particular" and recalled how her election heightened political awareness of her black constituents. "By and large Negroes had not known what a state senator or state representative did," Jordan explained. "Upon my election, there was an awaking to politics on the state level. This interest has encouraged people to follow the papers and become interested in the bills pending before the Legislature" (Bond 1968, 32). Other newly elected black officials in the South noted how their electoral wins raised hopes for improving services and economic conditions in black communities as well as encouraged other blacks to run for public office. Geneva Collins, who was elected as county clerk of Claiborne County, Mississippi, in 1967, observed that her successful bid for public office "seemed to give the Negro race the feeling that they had made the first step toward overcoming discrimination, poverty, and neglect in every arena." Thus, "they feel like they can progress, and this in itself made more people run for public office" (Bond 1968, 8).

The emerging black political empowerment in the post–civil rights era and its attendant effects on black civic participation were not confined to the South. Cities such as Chicago, Detroit, Los Angeles, and New York had black elected officials in local and state government as well as black representation in Congress before and during the civil rights movement, but demographic shifts in the 1960s and 1970s led to the election of more blacks to public office when these cities became increasingly black as whites departed for the suburbs. Political empowerment outside the South was symbolized by the election of blacks to mayorships during the late 1960s, 1970s, and 1980s in cities such as Flint, Cleveland, Gary, Detroit, Los Angeles, Oakland, Chicago, Philadelphia, Hartford, and New York, among many others.

These first-time campaigns to elect a black to the mayor's office often generated high levels of civic participation in northern black communities, as well as in southern cities such as Atlanta and New Orleans. For instance, William Nelson and Phillip Meranto, in their analysis of the 1967 campaigns of Richard Hatcher of Gary, Indiana, and Carl Stokes of Cleveland, Ohio, as the first black big-city mayors elected in the nation, note the "bandwagon effect" of black mayoral candidacies on black civic participation. They observed that these elections stimulated participation in the black communities of Gary and Cleveland in which "hundreds of volunteer workers – many of whom were grass-roots individuals with no previous experience in political campaigning" – were able to deliver the votes for Hatcher and Stokes (1977, 325).

The political incorporation of African Americans since the civil rights movement is also realized through activism in the Democratic Party. Blacks' loyalty to the Democratic Party, which was cemented during the 1970s and 1980s, has netted influence and some power in party policy and leadership (Smith 1990; Tate 1994; Smith 1996; but see Frymer 1999). Indeed, black delegates to the National Democratic Party have comprised nearly a quarter of all delegates to the convention since the mid-1980s (Joint Center for Political Studies 1988). Civil rights activist Fannie Lou Hamer and the Mississippi Freedom Democratic Party fought to be seated as delegates at the 1964 Democratic Convention, but by 1988 blacks sat on the Democratic National Committee's Executive Committee and served in large numbers on the party's Platform, Credentials, and Rules Committees. Indeed, 20 percent of the Platform Committee, the body responsible for shaping the policy perspectives of the party, was black, and the chair was then Representative William Gray III, who was also chairman of the powerful Budget Committee in the U.S. House of Representatives (Joint Center for Political Studies 1988).

Black influence in the Democratic Party was reflected in the phenomenal increase in black delegates to the party's national conventions. When the Mississippi Freedom Democratic Party contested the seating of the all-white delegation from Mississippi in 1964, there were only 65 black delegates seated at the convention, which represented less than 3 percent of all delegates (Jaynes and Williams 1989). By 1984 black representation at the convention had increased tenfold, accounting for nearly 18 percent of all delegates. The 1988 convention saw even greater growth. That year, 23 percent of all delegates to the convention were black, up considerably from 1984. A year later, Ron Brown became the first, and only, African American selected as chairman of the National Democratic Party. Brown would later become Secretary of the Commerce Department under the Clinton Administration, serving alongside the largest contingent of African Americans to ever be selected as presidential cabinet secretaries. Access and influence in the Democratic Party are a long way from the two seats offered to the Mississippi Freedom Democratic Party in 1964 and demonstrate blacks' incorporation into political institutions since the movement.

The political incorporation of blacks in the post–civil rights era is also evidenced by Jesse Jackson's 1984 and 1988 presidential bids. Even though the effectiveness of Jackson's campaigns have been debated by students of African-American politics (Reed 1986), the campaigns are considered to be critical moments in civic activism of African Americans in the post–civil rights era. Opinion surveys taken during the campaigns indicate surges in black civic engagement that at times exceeded the participation of whites. Indeed, in 1984 blacks were nearly twice as likely as whites to report attending political rallies and distributing campaign literature. Blacks were also three times more likely than whites to report helping others register to vote (Cavanaugh 1985).

ECONOMIC FORTUNES AND BLACK CIVIC ACTIVISM

Although the growth in the number of black elected officials, greater levels of access and influence in the Democratic Party, and the presidential bids of Jesse Jackson furthered the incorporation of African Americans into the mainstream of American politics, blacks' political empowerment has not been matched by black economic progress. Persistently high levels of black unemployment, surges in inflation, rising income disparities among blacks, growing levels of criminal victimization in black communities, and increased competition for low-wage and semiskilled jobs from influxes of immigrant workers reflect volatility in the economic and social fortunes of black communities at the same time that blacks were gaining political empowerment. These economic and social forces also have implications for understanding the dynamics of black political participation.

Students of black politics have noted Bayard Rustin's call for a tactical shift from protest to institutionalized politics, but students of black civic life have largely overlooked his prediction about transformations in the American economy and how those transformations might affect the future economic prospects of African Americans. Indeed, Rustin noted that the "greater problem" facing black communities would be the economic dislocation of a large segment of low-skilled and semiskilled black workers. As Rustin observed: "we are in the midst of a technological revolution which is altering the fundamental structure of the labor force, destroying unskilled and semiskilled jobs – jobs in which Negroes are disproportionately concentrated.... Whatever the pace of this technological revolution may be, the direction is clear: the lower rungs of the economic ladder are being lopped off." Moreover, Rustin predicted that class mobility in American life would be more difficult to attain and sustain. "An individual will no longer be able to start at the bottom and work his way up," Rustin predicted, "he will start at the middle or on the top, and hold on tight" (1971, 114).

Like his predictions about the transition from protest to electoral activism, Rustin's predictions about blacks' future position in the American economy might be equally as important to understanding the dynamics of black civic life in the post–civil rights era as advances in black political empowerment. Even though the black middle class has grown phenomenally since the 1960s, the black poor and an increasingly vulnerable black working class have suffered from declining economic fortunes and social decay in their communities.

Though the Great Society programs of the 1960s and early 1970s helped to lift many blacks out of poverty, about a quarter of blacks remain in poverty today. And while so-called ghetto neighborhoods prior to the civil rights movement included poor and working- and middle-class blacks within their boundaries, antidiscrimination housing laws and the economic progress of middle-class and stable working-class blacks have led to the concentration of poverty in inner-city neighborhoods and the departure of more affluent blacks to more economically stable communities outside of the inner city (Wilson 1980; 1987).

Indeed, by the late 1980s, rising economic inequality among blacks had become such a concern that veteran civil rights activists declared that the growing number of poor African Americans "casts a shadow over the gains made by the rest of society and by blacks themselves" (Joint Center for Political Studies 1987a, 1). Increasing social class divisions, they surmised, hampered collaborative political action across class lines in black communities. Their concerns highlight how growing class divisions among blacks put constraints on the ability of black organizations to coordinate civic and political action across black communities. As they note,

> the very success of our civil rights movement in reducing many barriers to education, employment, housing, and economic opportunity has created a gap in socioeconomic status between those blacks who were in the best position to seize new opportunities and those who were not, facilitating physical and economic separation. This new diversity within the black community has sometimes altered community structures, dispersed leadership, and diminished the capacity for cohesive, effective initiatives.
>
> (Joint Center for Political Studies 1987a, 9)

Growing class bifurcation has been noted in recent studies on black political life (Cohen and Dawson 1993; Dawson 1994a; Hochschild 1995; Harris 1999b). Michael Dawson notes that the "black community is literally divided into the haves and have-nots, those who have steady jobs and those who do not," arguing that this polarization influences the formation of black public opinion (Dawson 1994a, 43). Observing trends in black income distribution since the 1940s, Jennifer Hochschild notes that by the early 1990s economic polarization among blacks had widened to such a degree that "African-Americans are becoming more disparate politically and demographically as well as economically and socially" (Hochschild 1995, 48–50). Reviewing recent survey results, she also finds evidence of a latent rage and growing disaffection among middle class blacks that might have dire consequences for black activism (Hochschild 1998).

While political gains from the election of black elected officials and blacks' incorporation within the structure of the Democratic Party have empowered African Americans and presumably increased their participation in mainstream forms of political activities since the movement, economic indicators such as high levels of black unemployment and increasing levels of inequality *within* the black population raise questions about how black political empowerment and social and economic distress in black communities have altered black political activity since the movement. Simply put, how do these economic forces shape black civic participation in the post–civil rights era?

This book provides some answers. Our study on black civic activism is motivated by two perspectives in the literature on black politics: the black empowerment thesis (Browning, Marshall, and Tabb 1984;

Bobo and Gilliam 1990; Smith 1996; Leighly 2001) and perspectives on widening class polarization in black communities (Wilson 1980; Parent and Stekler 1985; Wilson 1987; Sigelman and Welch 1991; Cohen and Dawson 1993; Dawson 1994a; Hochschild 1995; Harris 1999b). As we have discussed, the black empowerment thesis posits that black candidacies and the election of blacks to public office increase levels of black participation and make blacks more interested in and aware of politics. In their study of the effects of black mayoralties on black social and political participation, Bobo and Gilliam note that they measure black empowerment as a feature of whether blacks have captured the mayor's office because "it involves the highest degree of *local* empowerment, usually signaling both high levels of organization among elites in the African-American community and a relatively high degree of control over *local* decision making" (1990, 379, emphasis added). Even though our definition of empowerment does not consider the decision-making power of black elected officials to assess black empowerment, our analysis, in contrast to other studies on black empowerment and its affects on black civic participation, takes a national perspective. Like previous studies of black empowerment and black participation, we consider the election of blacks to public office having a "bandwagon effect," where the electoral activities of black candidacies and the presence of blacks in public office increases and sustains black civic engagement.

In contrast to the positive effects of empowerment on participation, the class polarization perspective posits that growing class differences and poverty among blacks have implications for civic and political life in black communities (Wilson 1980, 1987; Cohen and Dawson 1993). For instance, Cathy Cohen and Michael Dawson (1993) find that the concentration effects of poverty dampen the civic and political participation of blacks living in poor neighborhoods. They find that the more African Americans live in high-poverty neighborhoods, the less likely they will engage in any form of political and social activity. With this concentration of poverty and its dampening effects on political participation, blacks across different class structures are less likely to share political resources and engage in cooperative political action. Thus, these concentration effects and their impact on participation raise questions about how rising inequality within the black population, as well as other economic and social indicators such as high levels of black unemployment, rising prices in goods and services, and labor competition affect changes in black civic activity over time.

COUNTERVAILING FORCES

Our theory of countervailing forces provides an alternative framework to the way that scholars have usually thought about the dynamics of black participation. Many important works in the field have tested the effects of black empowerment on black participation; however, few studies have explored how economic and social forces affect participation, and fewer still have simultaneously explored the impact of political empowerment and economic and social distress on black civic activism. In the tug-of-war between the force of empowerment and the potency of economic and social distress for the "soul" of black activism, we pinpoint how and which set of competing forces influences changes in black civic participation.

Consider the illustration of two black families from the popular television programs *Good Times* and *The Jeffersons*. While the upper-middle-class Jeffersons moved from a working-class community in Queens to Manhattan's plush Upper East Side, where they finally, as the show's theme song goes, get "a piece of the pie," the Evans family of *Good Times* were "scratching and surviving" in Chicago's notorious public housing project, Cabrini Green. The experiences of these two fictional families demonstrate how political and economic forces shaped their prospects for civic engagement in the post–civil rights era.

George Jefferson, whose fortune is made through a dry-cleaning business, opens his first store in 1968, the very day that Martin Luther King, Jr., is assassinated. As news circulates about King's death, the Jefferson's neighborhood erupts in violence and looting. By the mid-1970s, they find themselves living on New York's Upper East Side. Louise, George's wife, volunteers her time at the "Help Center," which is a crisis center for people who have fallen on bad times. She convinces George to hire a "street kid," helps write the center's newsletter, and receives awards for her volunteerism. George, whose motivations for civic engagement are usually shrouded with selfish intentions, joins an exclusive tennis club to meet potential clients, contacts the White House to invite President Carter to stay at his home during his next visit to New York, speaks to Harlem youth about his success as a black businessman, and secretly donates Christmas gifts every year to a family who lives in his boyhood apartment in Harlem. Their son Lionel attends college and later joins the family business. The world of the Jeffersons seems insulated from the economic and social realities of inflation, unemployment, and other conditions that could present obstacles to their civic engagement.

The Evans family has a different experience. In the mid-1970s, Florida and James Evans are living in a two-bedroom apartment in a high-crime public housing project with three children, Michael, Thelma, and J.J. James finds it difficult to find a steady job to support his family. Florida works at home but occasionally works outside the home to support her family. She attended night school to earn a high school equivalency diploma while her eldest son, J.J., barely graduates from high school. The family occasionally receives eviction notices because they cannot afford to pay the rent and is plagued by unemployment and rising prices. Indeed, things get so tough for one elderly neighbor, Gertrude, that she is suspected of eating pet food because she cannot afford groceries. The Evans family is also impacted by criminal activity in the community. Street gangs threaten J.J. and his younger brother Michael. Their father's solution to the unsafe conditions in the apartment building is to purchase a gun to protect the family.

Despite the economic and social hurdles of the Evans family, there are episodes of civic engagement. Alderman Fred Davis, though shady in his dealings, provides some access for the Evans family to have their grievances heard. On one occasion, the conditions in the building become so bad that the Evans kids and their neighbors circulate a petition to terminate the building superintendent. On another occasion the reelection of the Alderman Davis encourages intense political discussions in the Evans' household when James and J.J support Davis and Florida and Willona, a friend and neighbor, support his opponent. When Davis runs for reelection, he asks J.J. to speak at a campaign rally on his behalf (though he hands out an eviction notice when J.J. initially refuses). There are other examples of activism as well. Florida organizes a group of concerned citizens to boycott the local supermarket when her kids get food poisoning from spoiled meat, the family holds a fund-raising party for a neighbor whose electricity has been shut off for lack of payment, and Michael writes a letter to a local newspaper about the conditions in his family's apartment, which gets an immediate response from the housing authority.

In aggregating the experiences of these two families, we might find that economic and political forces have countervailing effects on their civic participation. Both households engage in some form of political activities. The affluent members of the Jefferson family are somewhat protected from social and economic distress in black communities given their social status and their spatial distance from depressed black neighborhoods, while the Evans family's political activities are likely conditioned by changes in their social and economic circumstances. In theory, the civic participation of both families is positively affected by the rising tide of black empowerment. Even though the black middle class has increased in size since the civil rights movement, most African Americans are placed somewhere between the Jeffersons and the Evans. Aggregating the civic activity of African Americans provides a profile of black civic engagement in which the competing forces of black empowerment and social and economic distress can be assessed. As factors that influence black civic life, black empowerment and economic and social distress may exhibit a "push and pull" on black civic activity, where empowerment pulls aggregate levels of black civic participation upward, while social and economic distress pushes aggregate levels of black civic participation downward. In aggregating black civic participation, our approach moves the focus away from established perspectives on black political life and political participation that emphasize micro-level, individualist explanations for political behavior such as education and income. We instead develop a theoretical perspective that highlights how structural constraints and opportunities in American politics and the American economy influence the contours of black civic activity.

A MACRO APPROACH

To test our theory of countervailing forces, we take a macro approach. Our theory contends that competing forces in the political, social, and economic environments influence shifts in black civic activism. Taking a macro approach is a departure from research on black political behavior as well as research on political participation. Using an approach that is more commonly recognized in the study of party identification and public opinion (Page and Shapiro 1992; Erikson, MacKuen, and Stimson 2002), we bring innovation to our study of black participation by aggregating the civic activities of blacks as a group. The first-order approach that scholars of political participation use to assess factors that influence participation is the socioeconomic status (SES) model. The SES model consistently demonstrates how individual attributes predict an individual's proclivity to engage in civic participation. From the perspective of the SES model, individuals are endowed with personal resources such as education and income that increase their participation.

In our analysis we make an analytical leap by moving from the individual as the unit of analysis to aggregated behavior as the unit of analysis. In doing so, we move beyond the standard SES model of participation by exploring the effects of macro-level economic, social, and political forces on aggregated measures of black civic activity. We argue that our macro approach provides a more theoretically and analytically consistent understanding of black civic activity as group behavior than studies that use individuals as the unit of analysis. By using macro-level economic, social, and political indicators to predict macro levels of black civic participation, our investigation of countervailing forces in black civic life will be analytically consistent and more suitable to our expectations about black political activity as a group phenomenon.

Taking this approach allows us to develop a dynamic rather than a static model of black civic participation. We examine changes in black civic participation from the beginning stages of black political incorporation in the early 1970s through the 1990s. We estimate the impact of changing economic and social conditions on black civic participation during this period as well. By developing aggregated measures of black civic participation over time, we are able to estimate how macro-level economic, social, and political forces affected black political activity over many years. Additionally, our macro approach allows us to go beyond the time-bound constraints of most empirical studies on black civic participation that examines behavior in a given year. Much has been gained through the analysis of the National Black Election Studies

(1984, 1988, 1996) and the 1993–1994 Black Politics Study, as well as other surveys with large samples of black respondents such as the 1982 and 1987 General Social Surveys.

These surveys and the studies that have been produced from them have expanded our understanding of the micro dynamics of black political behavior. Micro approaches, which dominate a subfield that is dedicated to explaining the political behavior of a racial group, examine how individual resources (such as income, education, age, gender), attitudes (such as partisanship, feelings of group solidarity, issue preferences, trust), and skill acquisition (such as involvement in churches and civic organizations) influence black participation (Tate 1991; Cohen and Dawson 1993; Dawson 1994a; Tate 1994; Verba et al. 1995; Harris 1999a). Unfortunately, these studies provide only a snapshot of black political participation in a moment in time. Instead of time-bound analyses of black political activity, our macro approach assesses aggregate-level movements in black civic participation during a period when African Americans gained unprecedented access and influence in mainstream American politics and where their economic and social fortunes as a group saw both progress and setbacks.

Using a macro approach and building on micro-centered scholarship on black empowerment and class polarization, our theory of countervailing forces allows us to answer questions that are only rarely empirically tested in the literature. On the empowerment side we ask: How have aggregate-level changes in the number of black elected officials over the years influenced aggregate-level movements in black civic participation? What difference does having a Democrat or Republican in the White House have on black civic participation? How much does having a viable black presidential candidate influence black civic participation? Have changes in the number of blacks going to college enhanced black civic participation over time?

On the social and economic distress side we ask: Do fluctuations in black unemployment alter aggregate-level movements in black civic activity? Does rising income inequality among blacks affect black civic participation in anyway? Do economic good times and bad times influence aggregate-level movements in black civic participation? Do surges or declines in the level of black criminal victimization influence black civic participation? And the question that is at the heart of this analysis: How do political empowerment and social and economic distress balance out as forces that affect black civic participation?

GROUP THEORY OF DEMOCRACY

For groups to have influence in the political process, they must participate in the workings of government. This is a major tenet of perspectives in democratic theory. Without sustained engagement in the political process, groups, and especially marginal groups, will not be able to elect representatives that reflect their political interests and preferences, nor will they be able to organize to voice their preferences more generally. In theory, groups that organize around their preferences, no matter their material condition, are supposed to level the political playing field, thereby closing the advantage that affluent groups have over less affluent groups in voicing their interests and preferences. However, as a generation of democratic theorists has argued, privileged groups have more resources at their disposal than disadvantaged groups to express their interests, and thus the playing field is unbalanced.

In their important work on political participation and civic voluntarism in the United States, Verba et al. (1995) show how the capacity to participate in civic and political activities is distributed differently across racial, ethnic, and gender categories. In some cases, resources such as time and politically enhancing civic skills are distributed equally across some social groups, while material resources such as money lean heavily toward the affluent. African Americans participate in religious institutions to a greater extent than whites and Latinos, providing them with politically relevant skills that enhance their political participation. But on the whole, the distribution of individual-level resources across groups demonstrates that whites (and particularly white males) have overall greater levels of money and skills to participate in civic and political activities than do African Americans and Latinos. These inequities in civic skills and resources strengthen the voices of the affluent and privileged in the political system and weaken the voices of those on the margins of society.

Although our macro model of black political participation does not directly address resource deficiencies in the black population over time, it does raise questions about how individual attributes that are likely to enhance black civic participation can be affected by the changing economic, social, and political fortunes of African Americans. Although time, money, and skills are important individual attributes for understanding why citizens become civically engaged, our theory of countervailing forces raises questions about the capacity of African Americans as a group to nurture and sustain politically relevant resources for civic participation given ever-changing economic and social conditions. Because downturns in the social and economic fortunes of black communities almost certainly contribute to declining employment opportunities and mobility and weaken the capacity of blacks to sustain materially community institutions that are vital to the development of civic skills, the ability of African Americans to stockpile politically relevant resources such as money and civic skills can be affected by volatility in the economic and social circumstances of blacks as a group.

Our theory of countervailing forces evolves from the existing literature on black empowerment and the intraclass polarization perspectives in black politics; consequently, this book focuses exclusively on black political behavior. Quite simply, our questions are motivated by debates within the black politics literature rather than perspectives on black–white differences in political participation. Micro-centered analysis of black political behavior has demonstrated that African Americans think about, perceive, and behave differently with respect to politics. The unique historical and contemporary political and economic experiences of inequality in America have shaped a worldview in black communities that is distinct from the experiences of other groups in the United States (Dawson 1994a; McClain and Steward 2002). Thus, we are cautious of adopting theoretical frameworks on black participation that strictly replicate research that derives from the behavior of the majority population (see Walton 1985 and Jones 1992). It may be true, nonetheless, that economic and social distress indicators that we explore in this study may influence the civic participation of whites and other minority groups. However, this is a question that is beyond the scope of this analysis because our theory is concerned with blending perspectives in the literature on black empowerment and distress in black communities and because our questions are aimed toward developing a profile of black civic life since the civil rights movement.

MEASURING BLACK CIVIC ACTIVISM

Like previous scholarship in political participation, our definition of civic activism encompasses participation beyond the voting booth and considers an array of activities that allow citizens to voice their concerns within the political system (Verba et al. 1995; Putnam 2000). The shift from protest to political incorporation drew energy away from movement activism toward mainstream acts of participation such as voting in local and national elections, contacting public officials, attending campaign rallies, and signing petitions in support or opposition to important issues influencing black people's lives. In developing a model to test our theory of countervailing forces, we examine *nonvoting civic participation*. The basis of excluding voting from our analysis is both practical and theoretical. From a practical standpoint, an analysis of black voter participation across time and place is hampered by the lack of comparable data on registration and turnout. Because voter registration laws vary by state and there are multiple elections occurring within a voting district, there are no year-to-year national estimates of voter participation and turnout in the United States. Consequently, we are unable to reliably estimate, in a continuous fashion, the simultaneous effects of black empowerment and economic and social distress on black registration and turnout using a macro approach. National estimates of voter registration are produced only for presidential election years and congressional midterm elections, but for no years in between.

From a theoretical standpoint, we are interested in nonvoting civic participation because it reflects grassroots activism. Individuals participate in civic and political activities in a variety of ways, from attending political rallies or working for a political party to serving as an officer in an organization or writing a letter about an issue to a newspaper. Unlike voting, engagement in nonvoting electoral participation and involvement in organizational life are demanding forms of civic engagement that require commitment beyond casting a ballot. These grassroots activities give voice to the political system when the voting booths are stored away until the next election. The acts of civic and political activities that are covered in our analysis can occur before, during, and after presidential, congressional, state, or local elections.

Exploring movements in these civic activities over the course of three decades provides an uninterrupted time line to assess the effects of political, macroeconomic, and social changes on black civic and political participation.

SOURCES OF THE DATA

We test our theory of countervailing forces on nonvoting electoral participation, organizational participation, and a composite measure of black civic participation. Our aggregate measures of black civic participation reflect grassroots activism and nonvoting electoral activities. In their study of black participation, Bobo and Gilliam use voting and nonvoting indicators of participation to estimate the effects of black empowerment on black participation. They combine electoral activities such as working in a campaign with activities like membership in civic groups to create a measure of "sociopolitical participation" (1990, see Appendix).

Even though the impact of black empowerment on nonvoting electoral participation may be obvious, its effect on black organization participation may appear less so. We speculate that black empowerment will influence black organizational participation for the same instrumental reasons that empowerment affects black electoral participation. Black empowerment may have a cascading effect on black organizational participation because it may send positive signals to civic actors indicating that their interest and concerns will be attended to by political elites. For instance, when a black president of the school board is elected, black citizens may be more willing to join the PTA, attend school board meetings, or participate in public forums about education policy.

Our analysis uses black respondents from the Roper Social and Political Trends data set, a collection of twelve survey questions on political participation that was asked repeatedly on a quarterly basis from 1973 to 1994. These questions explore a variety of civic activities, from attending a political rally or speech to working for a political party to signing a petition and to writing to a member of Congress. There are more than 400,000 respondents included in the cumulative file, and of those, more than 45,000 respondents are black. This wealth of data allows us to examine eighty-four continuous quarters of aggregate-level civic participation to assess the influence of macro-level factors on black nonvoting activity during a twenty-one-year period. We use government statistics on income disparities among black families (GINI index); black unemployment rates; and the rate of price inflation in goods, services, and production (price-deflated gross domestic product), yearly immigration rates, estimates of black crime victimization, and black college enrollment figures to assess aggregate-level movements in black participation. Information on the year-to-year numbers of black elected officials in the nation is gathered from the volumes of the *National Roster of Black Elected Officials*, a publication that has tracked the number of black elected officials since 1970.[1] As an indicator of black empowerment on a national level, the estimates reflect an aggregate measure of black empowerment on the local level since 70 percent of black public officials are elected to school boards, city councils, and county commissions.

STRUCTURE OF THE BOOK

We now return to the question that motivates our study: Are black empowerment and social and economic distress countervailing forces in black civic life? We begin our analysis in Chapter 2 by charting trends in the social, political, and economic conditions of African Americans in the post–civil rights era. Examining the economic and social trends that affect black America over the course of two and a half decades sets the stage for our analysis of whether there are countervailing forces affecting black political participation. Chapter 3 discusses the theoretical and analytical arguments of our macro framework for exploring black civic participation. Inspired by scholarship on macro political behavior and attitudes (Page and Shapiro 1992; Erikson, MacKuen, and Stimson 2002), we argue that even though scholars of black political behavior make claims about the political

[1] The annual census of black elected officials (BEOs) is collected by the Joint Center for Political and Economic Studies. It is the most reliable source of information on BEOs and as such it is routinely cited. The center uses a multilayered approach to estimate the number of BEOs. It uses telephone contacts with selected black officials and government or public bodies as well as a national clipping service to ascertain information about officials. Information on officials is organized by state, and the list of officials is mailed to secretaries of state, state election offices, and state school officers for review and verification.

behavior of African Americans as a group, our macro approach to black civic participation offers an alternative and analytically consistent model of black behavior. We argue that our macro perspective allows us to go beyond analyses drawn from a single year and enables us to assess black civic participation as group behavior rather than an artifact of individual behavior. We also trace quarterly level movements in various forms of black civic and political participation, providing us with a portrait of changes in aggregate levels of black participation in the post–civil rights era.

Chapter 4 steps back in time to examine the historical foundations of the ebb and flow of black civic participation from Reconstruction through the modern civil rights movement. Our historical analysis details the push and pull impact of economic, social, and political forces on black civic participation, showing how macro forces such as war, immigration, migration, industrialization, and partisan realignments shaped black civic participation over time. From this perspective we speculate on how changes in the economic, social, and political forces such as the rise in number of black elected officials, partisan changes in the presidency, inflation, and black unemployment affect movements in black civic participation. We also present our methodological justifications for using a generalized least squares (GLS) model to consider the time dynamics of our analysis.

In Chapter 5 we estimate the simultaneous effects of social, economic, and political forces on black civic participation, from 1973 to 1994. This analysis allows us to consider the impact of countervailing forces on macro-level movements in black participation over the course of three decades, giving us a block of time to weigh the relative effects of political, macroeconomic, and social forces on black participation. Our findings support our theory of countervailing effects across region, gender, and, to a lesser extent, social class. In summary, we find that the downward spiral in African-American economic and social fortunes swamps the participatory benefits that accrue from our measures of black political empowerment.

Chapter 6 concludes our analysis with a discussion of the contributions of our theory of countervailing forces and our macro approach for understanding the dynamics of black civic participation. We also discuss how a macro perspective on black participation can illuminate micro-centered explanations on black participation. We explain the implications of our findings, which suggest that economic vulnerability and social decay in black communities are far more important to explaining changes in black civic participation than black empowerment. If protest is not enough, as Browning, Marshall, and Tabb argued over two decades ago, then is black political empowerment enough to sustain black civic life given the retrogression in blacks' economic and social progress in the post–civil rights era?

Because civic and political participation is central to democracy in the United States, our theory of countervailing forces raises questions about how structural forces that are embedded in the American economy stifle the political voices of African Americans. As Lester Milbrath and M. L. Goel argued in their classic study, *Political Participation*, structural barriers to citizen participation undermine democracy, for "if a system presents barriers to participation for some people and eases the path to participation for others, these differences in opportunities to participate might be considered system defects which violate an important social norm for justice and equality" (1977, 152). Our theory of countervailing forces, therefore, leads us to question whether true political equality for African Americans can ever be accomplished without economic equality. In considering this question, we see our analysis of black civic participation as a step toward framing a larger discussion in American politics about how social and economic forces may diminish the civic participation of all Americans.

2

Good Times and Bad

Trends in the Economic, Social, and Political Conditions of African Americans in the Post–Civil Rights Era

> There's been so many things that's
> held us down,
> but now it looks like things are finally
> coming around.
> I know we got a long, long way to go,
> and where we'll end up,
> I don't know.
> But we won't let nothing hold us back,
> we're putting ourselves together,
> we're polishing up our act.
> If you ever been held down before,
> I know you refuse to be held down
> anymore.
>
> "Ain't No Stoppin' Us Now,"
> McFadden and Whitehead, 1979

The disco-influenced bass line of the 1970s anthem, "Ain't No Stoppin' Us Now," symbolizes the ups and downs of black progress in the post–civil rights era. As the decade of the 1970s neared its end, this popular tune came to express blacks' collective triumph over the adversities of the segregationist past. The tune also conveys feelings of an uncertain future for African Americans, despite some progress during the first full decade after the movement and a determination to never be held down again by racial oppression. The passage of the 1964 Civil Rights Act, the 1965 Voting Rights Act, and the 1968 Fair Housing Act expanded economic and political opportunities for African Americans as they pushed ahead to become players in the nation's economic and political mainstream. The transition from protest to institutionalized politics occurred in a short period of rapid change that accompanied the 1968 death of Martin Luther King, urban riots of the late 1960s, the rise and eventual fall of the black power movement by the early 1970s, and the 1972 Gary convention, which called for greater political and economic empowerment for blacks. By the early 1970s, African Americans were making gains in the political system, electing black mayors in such big cities as Atlanta, Detroit, and Newark, New Jersey, and sending blacks to Congress from districts as far west as Los Angeles and Oakland and as far south as Houston and Atlanta. After the marching slowed in the streets, blacks marched to the voting booths, enhancing their power in mainstream politics by electing their own to public offices. As one poster featured by a civil rights organization read during the 1970s: "Hands that once picked cotton can now pick presidents."

Since the civil rights movement, the march toward progress has yielded mixed results. While there have been tremendous gains in black political empowerment over the years, the economic and social progress of African Americans has been as bouncy as McFadden and Whitehead's base line. Though it is true, as Jennifer Hochschild notes, that "African-Americans are in many, but not all, ways better than their forebears were" (1995, 40), students of black civic and political life may be overlooking important economic and social forces that adversely affect blacks' full participation in the American polity. Indeed, these forces may be contributing to an unanticipated form of political inequality, an inequality that depresses the civic participation of African Americans despite the elimination of legal barriers and the progress made in electing blacks to public office. Although they are not the same as the legal barriers that once barred blacks' participation in the polity, structural barriers that derive from forces in the economy and society may be as effective barriers to civic and political life for many blacks as the legal barriers of the past.

This chapter introduces the economic, social, and political indicators that we will use to estimate aggregate-level movements in black activism over time. Because neither social nor economic forces are static entities, we examine changes in social, economic, and political indicators over the course of our study – from 1973 to 1994. We believe that these indicators have a bearing on black civic participation, either moving bundles of black civic activities upward or moving them downward. Using various types of indicators, we argue – and test more explicitly in succeeding chapters – that there are two sets of opposing forces affecting nonvoting black participation.

On one hand, indicators of black political empowerment – measured in our analysis by the actual number of black elected officials in a given year, the presence of a viable black presidential candidate, which party holds the presidency, and aggregate levels of black high school graduates attending college – should pull aggregate levels of black civic participation upward. On the other hand, indicators of social and economic distress – measured in this analysis by black income dispersion, black unemployment, inflation, immigration and black criminal victimization – may, depending on whether these indicators are trending in a negative direction, pull aggregate levels of black participation downward.

Our first step toward investigating our claims of countervailing forces is to see how economic, social, and political indicators have changed over the course of two decades. As the evidence in this chapter suggests, the post–civil rights era has been a period of good and bad times for African Americans where the good times point to enhanced political empowerment and the bad times reflect retrogression in many social and economic indicators.

TRENDS IN BLACK POLITICAL EMPOWERMENT

One of the most striking developments in the progress of African Americans since the civil rights movement is the emergence of black elected officials. Traditional civil rights organizations were the vanguard of black leadership before and during the movement, but black elected officials have, over time, developed a commanding presence in the politics of black communities. This presence, which is generated by black office-seeking and black office-holding, has been viewed as a force that enhances black civic participation. The mere existence of more black elected officials in the American polity has helped to secure the transition from protest activism to participation directed toward elections and constituency-oriented participation. Although black elected officials only represent 2 percent of all elected officials in the United States,

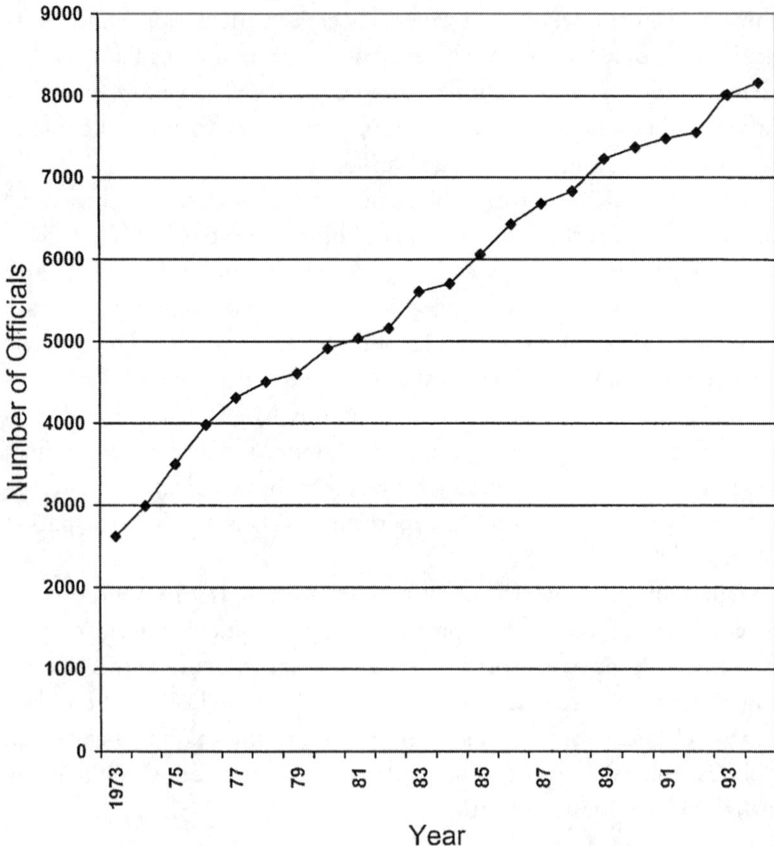

FIGURE 2.1. Annual number of black elected officials, 1973–1994. Source: Vital Statistics on American Politics

their impact on black civic participation should not be underestimated, especially since the overwhelming majority of black elected officials represents districts that are majority black or have black pluralities.

The sheer growth in black elected officials has been phenomenal. Since the Joint Center for Political and Economic Studies began its annual census of black elected officials in 1970, the number of blacks elected to public office has been steadily climbing. Figure 2.1 shows the actual number of black elected officials between 1973 and 1994. In 1973, there were about 2,600 blacks elected to public office across the country, nearly doubling their numbers since 1970. By 1983 the number of blacks in public office jumped to about 5,600, which doubled the number of officials in 1973. By 1994, there were more than 8,000 black elected officials, almost four times the number of BEOs that held office in 1973. Even though the number of black elected officials has gradually increased over time, the year-to-year percentage change in their numbers has dropped off precipitously since the early 1970s. Between 1971 and 1975, the percent increase in the number of BEOs fell from 25 percent to 18 percent. By 1979, the percent increase in the number of BEOs in the previous year was only 3 percent. Between 1980 and 1994, the percent change in BEOs hovered between 5 and 10 percent.

Most black elected officials have been elected to municipal offices (the overwhelming majority of which are city council seats) and to school boards. While previous work has used black mayorships as a marker of black political empowerment, most black elected officials serve in less visible positions. From 1973 to 1994, between 40 and 50 percent of BEOs were elected to municipal positions while 20 to 25 percent of BEOs served on school boards during this period. In estimating the effects of black political empowerment on black participation, we go beyond previous studies and use the actual number of black public officials as an indicator of black political empowerment.

We recognize that the election of black officials in a variety of offices may stimulate black civic participation in the aggregate. Black representation on city councils, county commissions, and school boards may enhance participation because the presence of BEOs may signal to blacks a more receptive political environment. A more receptive environment may stimulate black activism by persuading blacks to contact black local officials about a problem, by encouraging blacks to believe that their requests will be acted upon, and by energizing blacks to run in local races. On the other hand, the effects of black elected officials on black civic participation may also reach a threshold point. As the novelty of electing a black to public office wears off, the participatory effects of black office-holding and black office-seeking may also diminish with time.

THE PRESIDENCY AND BLACK CIVIC ACTIVISM

The overwhelming majority of black voters and elected officials are Democrats. Their incorporation in the party and the unwavering votes that blacks give to Democratic candidates should politically empower

African Americans during Democratic presidential administrations. Just as we see increases in the number of black elected officials expanding opportunities for blacks to become engaged in civic affairs, we also believe that a Democratic presidential administration may expand opportunities for black civic engagement because blacks are likely to perceive Democrats being more open to their policy preferences than Republicans.

In the period of our analysis, there are two Democratic administrations: Jimmy Carter's term (1977–1980) and the first year of Bill Clinton's first term (1993–1994). For most of the years in our analysis, four Republican administrations are in office: one year of Nixon's second term (1973–1974), Ford's completion of Nixon's term (1974–1976), Reagan's two terms (1981–1988), and Bush's term (1989–1992). In general, Democratic administrations were more supportive of positive civil rights policies and social welfare programs than Republican administrations. Additionally, Democratic administrations appointed more blacks to cabinet positions than Republicans, reflecting blacks' growing incorporation into the party.

For instance, Carter appointed blacks to high-profile positions such as the Secretary of Housing and Urban Development (Patricia Roberts Harris) and the United States' representative to the United Nations (Andrew Young) during his administration. He also made important black appointments in areas of civil rights, such as the chairmanship of the Equal Employment Opportunity Commission (Eleanor Holmes Norton), solicitor general (Wade McCree), and assistant attorney general for civil rights (Drew Days). Though many black leaders raised questions about whether blacks were getting their fair share of appointments as the most loyal constituency of the Democratic Party and criticized Carter for not giving enough support to social welfare policies, the Carter administration was more receptive to civil rights and social welfare policies than either the Nixon or Reagan administrations (O'Reilly 1995).

In contrast to the expanding opportunities to engage in policy-directed participation under a Democratic administration, Republican administrations provided diminishing opportunities for blacks to have their policy preferences acted upon. Despite Nixon's support of affirmative action through the Philadelphia Plan – which called for goals and timetables in hiring blacks in government-subsidized construction jobs – and his support for a guaranteed income for the poor, the Nixon administration was hostile to civil rights policies. This hostility was mostly expressed in the administration's opposition to busing, which federal courts had mandated as a remedy to racially desegregate public schools. Nixon's administration refused to terminate federal funding to school districts that practiced racial discrimination as mandated by Title VI of the 1964 Civil Rights Act and further attempted to diminish civil rights gains by nominating conservative federal judges to the bench, including William Rehnquist to the Supreme Court (O'Reilly 1995, 300).

The Reagan presidency would continue the retrenchment policies that had gutted social welfare policies and weaken the enforcement of civil rights laws that began under the Nixon administration. Reagan used racially tinged codes to convey his opposition to civil rights and social welfare programs, adopting, for instance, terms such as "welfare queens" to symbolize abuses in the welfare system. In one of his first presidential campaign speeches, which took place in Philadelphia, Mississippi, the town known for the death of three civil rights activists in 1964, Reagan emphasized the importance of states' rights over federal policies. Federal civil rights policies, such as the 1965 Voting Rights Act, had been crucial to enforcing civil rights of southern African Americans during the 1960s and 1970s. Furthermore, the Reagan administration appointed arch-conservatives such as Edwin Meese, who served as attorney general, and William Bradford Reynolds, who served as assistant attorney general for civil rights. Their approach to civil rights policies attempted to weaken long-held views on civil rights and voting rights. Indeed, civil rights enforcement slowed under the Reagan administration, and, like Nixon, Reagan appointed conservative judges to the federal bench, including Antonin Scalia to the Supreme Court. He also nominated Rehnquist to chief justice of the Supreme Court. African Americans were so opposed to the Reagan administration that over three-quarters of blacks reported in an opinion poll that they personally thought that the president was racist (Harris and Williams 1986).

Although Democratic presidential administrations might stimulate black participation because of expanding opportunities to have blacks' policy preferences addressed, Republican presidential administrations could stimulate black participation for a different reason. As blacks come to perceive Republican administrations as a threat to their policy preferences, blacks will become more active in civic affairs under Republican administrations than under Democratic administrations because threats to policies on civil rights and social welfare would mobilize African Americans in opposition to Republican administrations.

JACKSON PRESIDENTIAL CAMPAIGNS

In addition to our argument that Democratic presidential administrations are linked to the political empowerment of African Americans, we also consider the 1984 and 1988 presidential campaigns of Jesse Jackson as events that enhanced the political empowerment of African Americans in the post–civil rights era. Like the impact of black office-seeking and black office-holding on stimulating black civic participation, many analysts of the Jackson campaigns noted the increased levels of black voter registration and turnout as a result of his presidential run. Even though there have been debates about whether Jackson's campaigns strengthened the influence of blacks within the Democratic Party or within American politics more generally (Reed 1986), certainly Jackson's campaigns may have had the same bandwagon effect on black civic participation as black mayoral candidacies. For example, in his discussion of black presidential politics, Ronald Walters (1988) suggests that the legitimacy of Jackson's campaign for president was an important element in understanding black political participation. Because Jackson's presidential bid was taken seriously by many blacks and whites throughout the country, it is fair to say that his campaign may have served as a signal of the new types of political opportunities that were becoming available to African Americans in an era of increasing black political progress. Although some black leaders disagreed about whether blacks should collectively rally around an African-American candidate or advance their interests by supporting another candidate with a realistic chance of becoming president, it is clear that Jackson's status as a serious presidential contender marked a new level of political success that blacks had achieved after the civil rights movement. Thus, Jackson's campaign empowered African Americans to participate in civic affairs because his presence on primary ballots served as a signal to blacks that their political concerns might finally be addressed at the highest levels of American government. As campaigns that stimulated black political activism, we ask whether Jackson's runs in 1984 and 1988 had the same effects on non-voting civic activities. Considering the effects of Jackson's campaigns on civic participation will also allow us to estimate whether his presidential bids had a short-term, long-term, or negligible effect on black civic engagement.

EDUCATION AS A RESOURCE FOR POLITICAL EMPOWERMENT

A more indirect indicator of black empowerment in the post–civil rights era is the year-to-year change in the number of African Americans attending college. Education is one of the most consistent predictors of civic participation; cosequently, surges and declines in blacks attending college may affect aggregate levels of black civic activism. Education is important to participation because it lowers the material and cognitive costs associated with involvement in American civic life. Citizens who have higher levels of formal education know how the political system works, are socialized with norms that encourage interest and engagement in civic life, develop skills that can be transported to civic and political activities, and are more likely to follow current events, which leads to participation (Conway 2000, 27).

As a collective political resource for African-American communities, education is equally important for explaining aggregate-level shifts in black civic activism. In particular, we argue that aggregate levels of black college enrollment serve as an indicator of black political empowerment in black communities. As we noted earlier, the civic and political participation literature clearly stresses the importance of citizens' level of education for processing information necessary for engagement in civic affairs. Consequently, in our analysis, the aggregate percentage of black high school graduates that enroll in colleges or universities in a given year provides us with an empirical basis for gauging the information-processing capacity of black communities at specific moments in time. We use this aggregate-level indicator of education as a proxy for measuring how well blacks as a group can sort through the complexities involved in becoming active in civic activities. Although this perspective on the role of education is not new to students of political behavior, its aggregate-level interpretation is less commonly utilized in the civic participation literature. Thus, our readers might benefit from having these same ideas presented in a slightly different manner.

In our countervailing forces theory of black civic participation, we think of educational advancements as "human capital" improvements for African Americans as a group. Drawing from the human capital literature in economics we argue that receiving a postsecondary education transforms blacks into more productive and efficient consumers of social and political information, and, at the aggregate level, these enhancements lead to greater levels of black civic activism. According to Becker, human capital analysis, "assumes that schooling raises earnings and productivity mainly by providing knowledge, skills and a way of analyzing problems" (Becker 1993, 19). In the language of economics, we contend that increases in human capital endowments within black communities will lead to higher levels of black civic participation because African Americans as a group will be better able to understand and manage the complexities of civic engagement in an efficient manner. Thus, educational advancement functions as a source of black political empowerment because college attendance equips blacks with new knowledge that empowers and facilitates their collective participation in a variety of civic activities. Put another way, we utilize *aggregate* measures of black college enrollments as a proxy for the collective levels of human capital investments that black communities benefit from in a given time period.

Based on these ideas, we argue that as the percentage of black high school graduates who attend college increases, so should aggregate-levels of black civic participation. Conversely, as the number of blacks going on to college decreases, aggregate levels of black participation should decrease as well. Unlike the year-to-year number of black elected officials, the proportion of black high school graduates attending colleges has fluctuated over the past twenty-one years.

As Figure 2.2 shows, between 1973 and 1976, the proportion of black high school students going to college was slightly greater than 40 percent, with a surge toward 50 percent in 1977. However, the gains that were made in black high school graduates attending college were eroding by the early and mid-1980s. In 1982, 1985, and 1986, the rate dips below 40 percent, the lowest point in the twenty-one-year period of our analysis. Major cuts in student financial aid during the Reagan

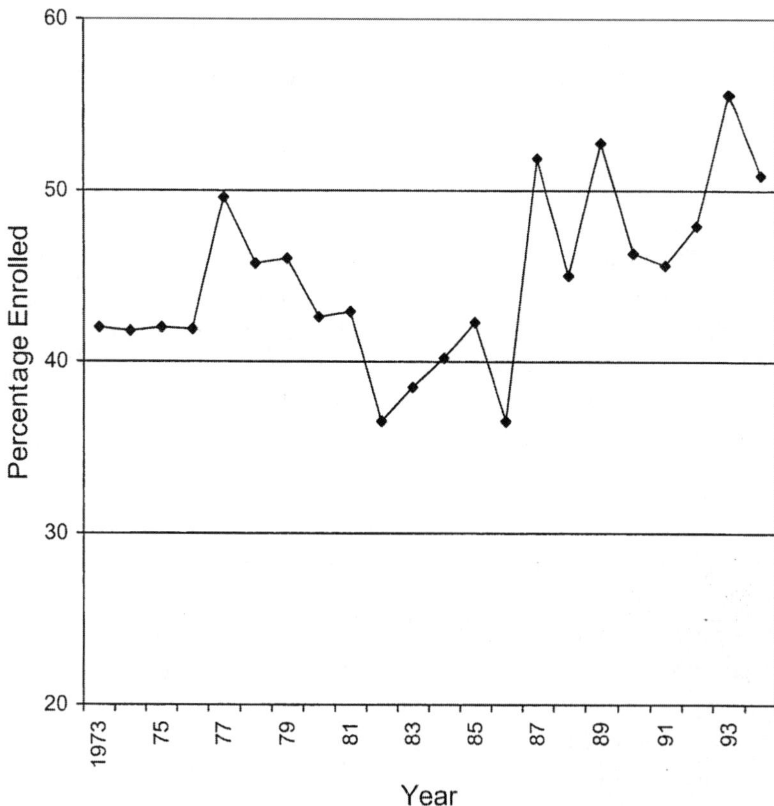

FIGURE 2.2. Annual college enrollment of black high school graduates, 1973–1994. Source: Digest of Educational Statistics

administration, which disproportionately affected black students, and the economic recession of the early 1980s partly account for the decline during that period. However, by the late 1980s, the number of black high school graduates entering college rebounds, where the college-going rate hovers around 50 percent and jumps to 55 percent in 1993, the highest rate during the period.

In addition to increases in blacks graduating from high school and the narrowing of education disparities between blacks and whites in secondary education, blacks improved their rate in the percentage of high school students going to college by 10 percent between 1973 and 1994. This improvement should boost the civic participation of blacks in the aggregate.

TRENDS IN ECONOMIC AND SOCIAL DISTRESS

Even though political empowerment indicators suggest that African Americans have made strides in becoming empowered in mainstream politics – whether it is measured in the number of blacks elected to public office or increases in politically relevant resources such as education – changes in social and economic circumstances indicate a mixed record of progress. Growing class inequality, periods of rising prices in goods, services, and production in the American economy, high levels of black unemployment, growing competition for low-wage jobs from immigrants, and spikes in crime victimization among blacks may be forces that have shifted aggregate levels of black civic participation downward.

BLACK INCOME INEQUALITY AND BLACK ACTIVISM

One indicator that captures changes in the economic circumstances of blacks as a group is income dispersion within the black population. This measure captures the level of economic bifurcation in the black population and reflects changes in the proportion of blacks in poverty, the erosion of wages among poor and working-class blacks, and the expansion of the black middle class into high-paying white-collar professions. As analysts of black political life are beginning to notice more and more, economic polarization is leading to political polarization in black communities. We see rising inequality within the black population as a force that depresses black civic participation. As income inequality widens in the black population, aggregate levels of black participation will shift downward because bifurcation will diminish the capacity of black political and civic organizations to coordinate political mobilization across class lines.

As early as the 1960s, when opportunities began to expand for blacks who had the wherewithal to benefit from emerging economic opportunities, analysts began to notice the widening gap in the economic opportunities of African Americans, speculating how social class differences would have political consequences for black politics. Observing the problems facing newly elected black officials, Kenneth Clark, in 1967, cited rising class divisions as one of those problems. "The fact that in the present doldrums of the civil rights movement the cleavages between the masses of Negroes and middle-class Negroes have become more clear and exacerbating," Clark observed, "the masses of Negroes are now starkly aware that recent civil rights victories, benefitted, primarily, a very small percentage of middle-class Negroes while their predicament remained the same or worsened" (1972, 156).

Questions about the political consequences of economic divisions in black communities would emerge again during the 1980s. Influenced by William Wilson's work on the urban underclass and the increasing mobility of the black middle class, students of black politics were asking whether widening class divisions among blacks influenced black political behavior. In an analysis of black political attitudes across social class, Wayne Parent and Paul Stekler (1985) found that middle-class blacks exhibited stronger feelings of racial group solidarity, were less likely to believe that the police treated black people as fairly as whites, and were less likely to think that blacks should receive help from the government. The authors attributed these differences to growing income differences between blacks and noted the potential consequences of the division for black electoral politics:

> There are potential splits in the black community though, that can be associated with differences in income. As more and more of the predominately black urban areas of the United States elect blacks to office, future elections in those places will feature fields of candidates who are mostly or completely black, and it is inevitable that splits in the black electorate will occur.
> (Parent and Stekler 1985, 533)

Michael Dawson (1994a) also finds class differences in black political attitudes. In explaining the homogeneity of blacks' political party identification and other political attitudes, Dawson argues for a theory of "linked fate," where individual blacks decide their political preferences based on whether policies and political parties are good for the group rather than for individual blacks. However, Dawson does find evidence of class divisions in some aspects of black public opinion. Most African Americans support measures to redistribute wealth in American society, but middle-class African Americans are less supportive of redistribution. And most African Americans are opposed to radical notions of black nationalism, but lower-income blacks are more likely to support radical nationalism than the rest of the black population (Dawson 1994a, 199).

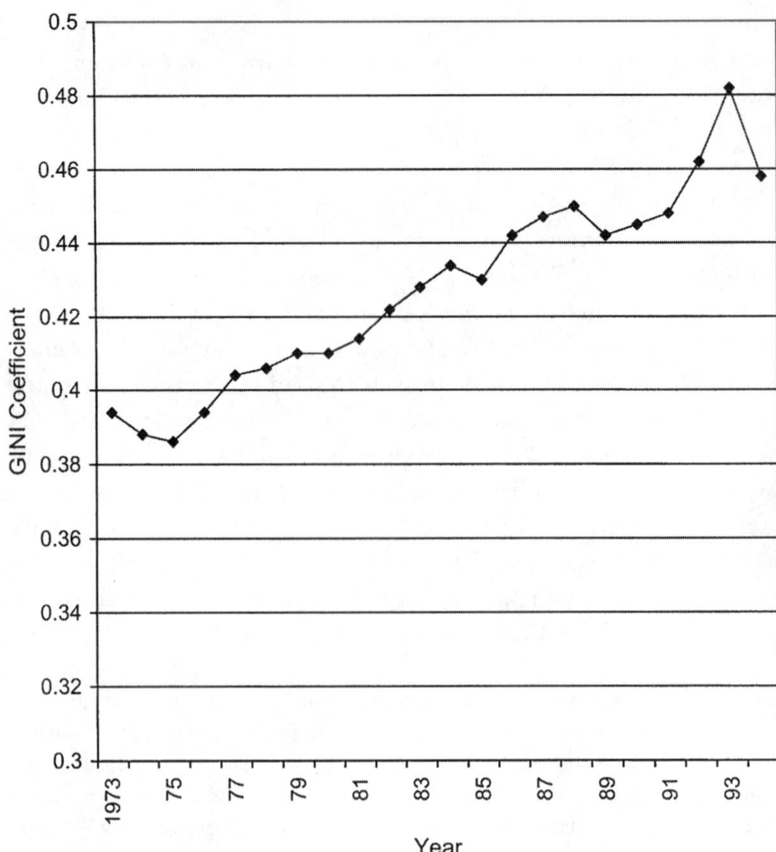

FIGURE 2.3. Black family income dispersion (GINI index), 1973–1994. Source: Current Population Survey

To capture the effects of income inequality among blacks in our macro approach to black participation, we use the GINI index, a measure used to estimate the degree of income inequality within a group or society. The index, which ranges from zero to one, indicates how equal or unequal income or wealth is distributed within a particular population. A value of zero indicates that there is perfect distribution of income in the population, while a value of one indicates that only a small fraction of people within the group command the group's share of income – a score of perfect inequality.

Figure 2.3 shows the degree of black family income dispersion for each year between 1972 and 1994. Although substantial inequality in income remains a reality between blacks and whites, the rate of inequality is growing faster within the black population. Black family income was more equitably distributed in the early 1970s, but since then income inequality among blacks has been on a steady climb. Inequality increases sharply during the late 1980s and makes a leap in the early 1990s. By the early 1990s, black middle-class families commanded a greater share of the income of all black families than they did twenty years earlier.

There are several reasons for the increase in income inequality within the black population. The growing number of African Americans in poverty, the decreasing economic opportunities for poor and working-class black men, the emergence of female-headed households plagued by poverty, the decline of stable skilled and semiskilled manufacturing jobs in the American economy, the decline in wages for working poor and working class, and the expanding opportunities of college-educated blacks have contributed to growing economic bifurcation among African Americans in the past three decades (Freeman 1976; Farley 1984; Sigelman and Welch 1991). As economist Martin Carnoy notes of the changing economic circumstances of poor/working-class blacks as opposed to middle-class blacks in the post–civil rights era:

> [T]he fall in black fortunes after the mid-1970s, and especially after 1979, was tied mainly to a decline in the incomes of low-income black households, where, almost by definition, part-time work was the rule rather than the exception. The black middle-class expanded slightly in the 1980s and their average income continued to increase. They, like their white counterparts, became ever more separated from the poor. (1994, 22)

Deepening class division may have a variety of effects on black civic participation. Such divisions would make it difficult for black communities to share and coordinate material resources that are important to individual and collective action, especially resources such as social networks and indigenous institutions that draw people into civic and political action. Even though poor and working-class blacks remain in communities where institutions and networks are weakening, middle-class blacks who live outside of traditional black communities may have weaker links to networks and institutions or create new ones that are exclusive of inner-city communities. So while the black middle class grows, the traditional networks and institutions that bonded blacks across social classes in the past may be weakening. If this is true, then growing inequality should push aggregate levels of black civic activism downward, despite the growing ranks of the black middle class.

BLACK UNEMPLOYMENT AND PARTICIPATION

Another indicator of social distress that may influence changes in the aggregate levels of black civic engagement is the rate of black unemployment. High levels of joblessness among African Americans have been a problem for decades where the rate of unemployment has been consistently above that of whites. As a rule of thumb, black unemployment has always been double or more than white unemployment, which demonstrates how bad economic times disproportionately affect African Americans. Not only do African Americans have considerably higher rates of unemployment than whites, but they are also more likely to be disproportionately represented among the underemployed, individuals who are so discouraged by the lack of job opportunities that they no longer seek employment. These jobless workers are not counted among the unemployed.

Figure 2.4 shows the unemployment rate of African Americans from 1973 to 1994. In the twenty-one-year period, high rates of black unemployment paralleled periods of economic recession. Black unemployment reached nearly 15 percent during the recession year of 1975 and gradually declined to 12 percent by the end of the decade. But already-high levels of black unemployment were on a decline, and by the early 1980s, black unemployment exceeded the rate that occured in the recession of the mid-1970s. By 1981, black unemployment exceeded 15 percent and jumped to nearly 20 percent in the recession years of 1982 and 1983. Black unemployment does not level off to its pre-1979 rate until the late 1980s. There is an increase in black unemployment during the recession of the early 1990s, but the rate does not reach the astronomically high rates of the early 1980s.

In their analysis of the impact of unemployment on political participation, Kay Lehman Schlozman and Sidney Verba argue that unemployment may affect individual political participation in two ways. Examining the political attitudes and participation of employed and unemployed, they speculated that the experience of unemployment "might have the direct effect of raising participation by giving the

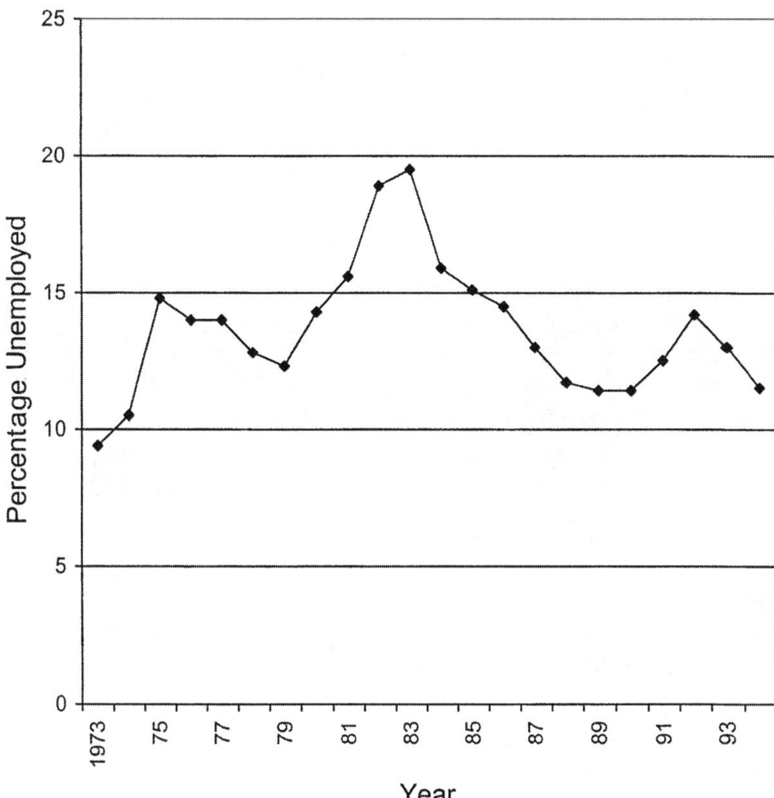

FIGURE 2.4. Black unemployment rate, 1973–1994. Source: Economic Report of the President

unemployed an incentive for activity and the extra time in which to be active," or it might have the opposite effect of reducing participation of the unemployed because "the pressures of looking for work and generating resources preclude other commitments, or because the unemployed are so debilitated psychologically that they withdraw from social and political life" (1979, 236). They find that being unemployed does not have an effect on political participation and that socioeconomic status rather than employment status has more of a bearing on political participation.

However, our expectation is that unemployment will have relevance for our macro model of black civic participation. Although we do not consider the effects of unemployment on individual levels of civic participation among blacks, the macro effects of black unemployment on aggregate levels of black civic engagement may be a significant force in explaining upward or downward shifts in black civic participation. From the perspective of our macro model of civic participation, rising rates of unemployment among blacks should depress aggregate levels of black civic participation because blacks, as a group, would have fewer material resources to devote to civic activism.

INFLATION AND BLACK CIVIC ACTIVISM

The state of the American economy over time may also influence aggregate-level movements in black civic participation. Like the percentage of blacks unemployed in a given year, we see rising prices in consumer goods and the cost of production (inflation) as a force that may influence the movements in aggregate levels of black participation. Higher prices for goods, services, and production affect all segments in society. Inflation contributes to economic distress and reflects the state of a sluggish economy, disproportionately affecting marginal communities throughout the society. Rising prices, especially in combination with high levels of unemployment, can be devastating for black communities because blacks are more affected by unemployment than whites and have fewer material resources to buttress the shock of higher living expenses.

Figure 2.5 shows the percentage change in price-deflated gross domestic product (GDP) for every year between 1973 and 1994. The percentages measure increases in the price of goods, services, and production from the previous year. As the figure demonstrates, inflation was a serious problem during the mid-1970s and early 1980s, two periods when the American economy suffered severe recessions. The rate falls to about 6 percent in 1982 and then to 4 percent in 1983. Afterward, yearly price increases are stable, sliding to about 2 percent in 1986, but slightly rising between 1987 and 1990. By the early 1990s, inflation declined gradually, hitting a low of almost 2 percent in 1994. Thus as a force that contributes to social distress, we see high levels of inflation indirectly depressing aggregate levels of civic participation by decreasing the material well-being of African Americans, thereby providing less material resources to sustain networks and institutions, which are critical to connecting citizens to civic and political action.

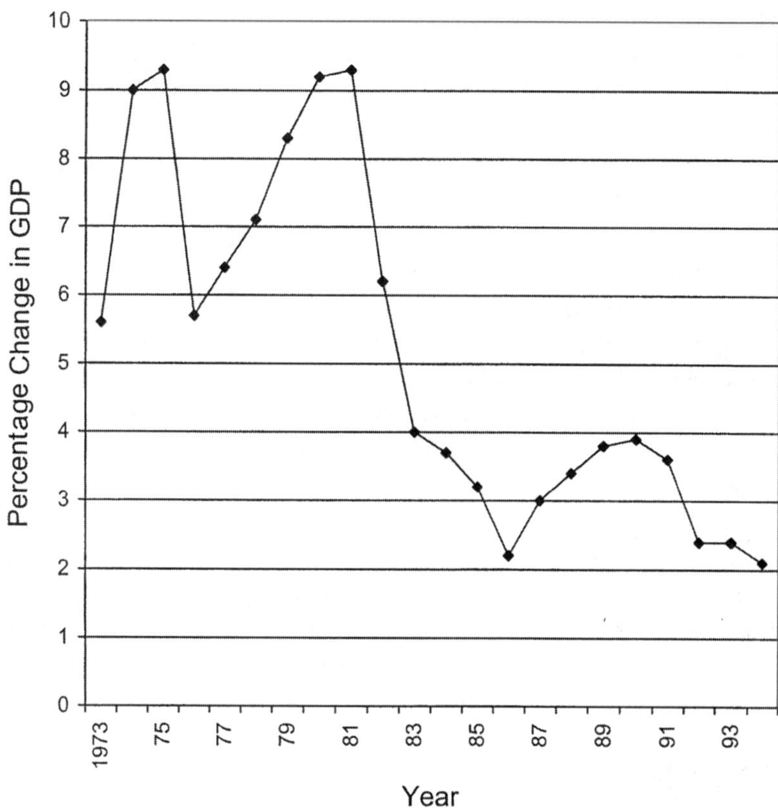

FIGURE 2.5. Rate of inflation (price-deflated GDP), 1973–1994. Source: Current Population Survey

IMMIGRATION, ECONOMIC COMPETITION, AND BLACK CIVIC ACTIVISM

Another form of social distress we consider are the economic consequences of immigration. We do not see immigration itself as a factor influencing aggregate levels of black civic participation, but rather we see the economic by-product of immigration as a force affecting aggregate-level movements in black participation. Immigration contributes to competition in low-wage and middle-wage occupational sectors and lowers the wages of native unskilled and semiskilled workers. Because black workers are disproportionally represented in those sectors, they are more likely to be affected by the economic consequences of rising immigration in the United States. African Americans made economic gains during the 1920s, when immigration controls were put into force and demand for industrial labor in northern cities was high. Nevertheless, racial discrimination prevented blacks from fully gaining economically from low immigration and the expansion of industrial jobs. As William Wilson explains of this period: "Immigration laws kept the flow of eastern and southern European immigrants to a mere trickle, thereby forcing industrialists to tap the industrial reserve of Negroes for unskilled labor" (1980, 68). However, "organized white-worker resistance, reinforced by norms of racial exclusion that crystallized with the emergence of Jim Crow segregation, effectively prevented the free employment of black labor in industry" (1980, 71).

Blacks made further economic gains in the post–World War II expansion of the American economy as more industrial jobs opened up better employment opportunities, increased their earnings, and further facilitated their migration from the dependency of the southern agrarian economy (Jaynes and Williams 1989). Thus the post–World War II economic gains of blacks were made because of a tight labor market, a plentiful supply of cheap labor, and little to no competition from low or semiskilled immigrants. As one economist observed of the progress blacks had made in the postwar period: "for twenty-five years, blacks were the major new source of low and semiskilled industrial labor" in the economy (Carnoy 1994, 86).

Just when black economic progress was being made and civil rights restrictions were being lifted, government immigration policies were also being altered. The year after the 1964 Civil Rights Act, which legally eliminated racial discrimination in public life, Congress passed the 1965 Immigration Act, which ended discrimination that gave preferential treatment to European immigrants over immigrants from developing counties. Discriminatory practices in national origin were replaced by rules that put a premium on family unification and the occupational skills of entrants, which opened immigration to individuals from developing nations, many of whom are low- and semiskilled workers.

Although it is difficult to make generalizations about the economic opportunities available to all recent legal and undocumented immigrants, some scholarly accounts suggest that many of these individuals find employment in service sector and other low-skill job settings, "including day labor, construction, and the textile industry" (DeSipio and de la Garza 1998, 51–3). At the same time, however, a large number of these jobs are also being sought after by African Americans. Thus, an expanding service sector labor force and increased competition for low- and semiskilled jobs raise questions about the possible civic and political implications of immigration in the post–civil rights era. For example, how might these forces indirectly affect the material resource (and consequently civic resource) base of African Americans as a group? In the sections that follow, we further develop our immigration argument by stating what we believe (and do not believe) about how immigration ultimately influences aggregate-level movements in black civic involvement.

To start, it is well known that material resources, such as household income levels, are key explanatory factors for understanding black civic participation. In short, African Americans who have higher incomes and greater wealth assets are more likely to participate in various civic activities. Consider, however, that structural forces (such as increasing immigration rates) may have an indirect, negative effect on the level of participatory resources that African Americans possess as a group. Thus, we argue that the economic consequences of increasing rates of immigration (lower earnings for some native blacks) negatively affect aggregate levels of participatory resources that are available to black communities.

It is important to note that scholars who study the economic effects of immigration generally find that there are modest, but significant, negative effects of an increasing immigrant labor supply on the earnings of African Americans in low- and semiskilled jobs (Muller and Espenshade 1985; Borjas 1987; Altonji and Card 1991; Lalonde and Topel 1991; Borjas 1998). Although these depressing effects may seem small at the individual level, our aggregate-level analysis suggests that African Americans as a group may indirectly experience some unfavorable civic and political consequences of immigration. Thus, even though individual black citizens may not directly "feel" the effects of small changes in their earnings at the individual level, the sum of these slight changes for the entire African-American population could be substantial and significantly influence aggregate levels of black civic participation.

We should also provide a point of clarification. We do not claim that labor market competition between blacks and new immigrant groups is strictly a zero-sum game. In fact, economists have demonstrated that new immigrants can be both substitutes and complements to production in a given labor market (Borjas 1987, 1998). However, we contend that although immigrants may not compete with blacks for jobs in every sector of the economy, enough evidence exists for us to argue persuasively that substantial numbers of African Americans who work in service sector industries may be adversely affected by increasing immigration rates. Our civic participation model incorporates these insights to explain changes in aggregate levels of black civic engagement in the post–civil rights era. To assist in this task, we examine trends in the rates of immigration to the United States since the modern civil rights movement.

Figure 2.6 shows the rate of immigrants per 1,000 inhabitants in the United States from 1973 to 1994. The immigration rate, which hovered around 2 percent, was steady between 1973 and 1977. There is a short bounce upward in 1978, reaching near 3 percent, but a bounce back to 2 percent in 1979. Between 1980 and 1988, the immigration rate remains stable, hovering around 2.5 percent. In 1989, the immigration rate begins a steep climb, reaching 4.5 percent in 1989, to more than 6 percent in 1990, to above 7 percent in 1991. It drops precipitously in 1992, to just under 4 percent and declines gradually in 1993 and 1994, when the rate nears 3 percent.

CRIMINAL VICTIMIZATION AND BLACK CIVIC ACTIVISM

Our final indicator of social distress is the changing rate of crime victimization among blacks. We use black crime victimization rates as a barometer for the level of social decay facing black communities at a given moment in time. Like our other social and economic indicators, periods of increases or decreases in criminal victimization may have different effects on aggregate-level movements in black participation. In his analysis of neighborhood responses to criminal activity, Wesley Skogan proposes a question that is important to our analysis of the effects of black criminal victimization on black civic activity: Does increasing crime "goad (citizens) into action, or do they give up in the face of mounting problems?" (1990, 65).

As a by-product of poverty and the lack of economic opportunities, violent criminal activities in black communities have affected the

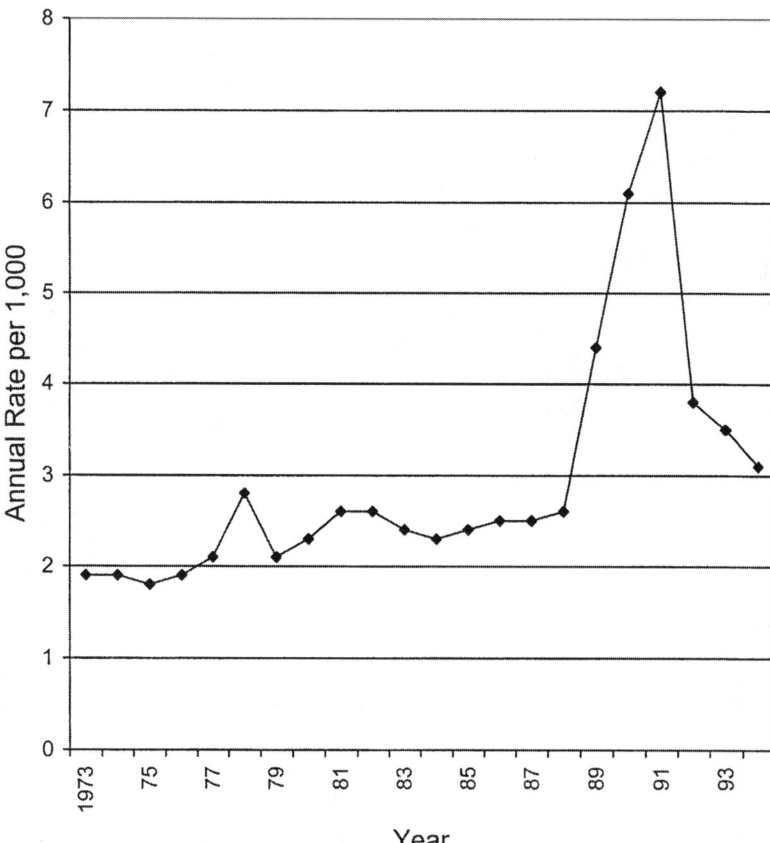

FIGURE 2.6. Immigration rate, 1973–1994. Source: Statistical Yearbook of the Immigration and Naturalization Service

black poor, working class, and even the black middle class (Pattillo-McCoy 1999). As with immigrant communities in American cities for most of the nineteenth and early twentieth centuries, poverty and discrimination are incubators of criminal activity in inner-city communities. The existence of poverty and the influx of drug trafficking in poor and working-class communities since the civil rights movement have had a direct impact on the quality of life in black communities. Criminal activity leads to disorder in urban communities, an atmosphere that "undermines the mechanisms by which communities exercise control over local affairs," and it further discourages civic and political action because crime "fosters social withdrawal,

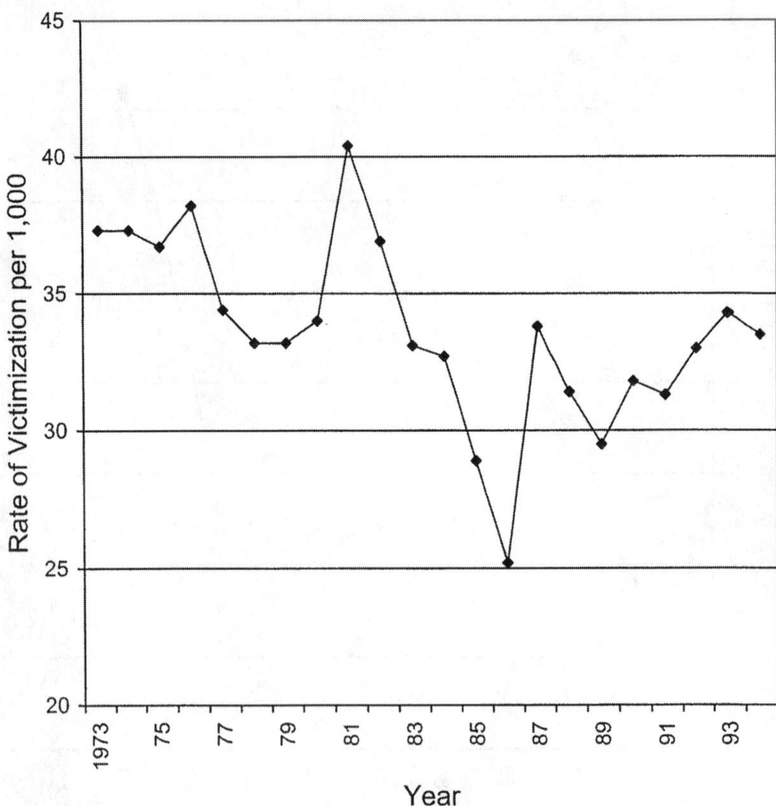

FIGURE 2.7. Criminal victimization of blacks, 1973–1994. Source: Bureau of Justice Statistics

inhibits cooperation between neighbors, and discourages people from making efforts to protect themselves and communities" (Skogan 1990, 65).

Figure 2.7 shows the rate of criminal victimization for African Americans between the early 1970s and 1990s. Except for a peak in the early 1980s, blacks have become less victimized by crime over the twenty-one-year period. However, there are clearly periods when African Americans were more likely and less likely to be affected by crime. In the early 1970s, about 38 of every 1,000 African Americans were victimized by a crime. Between 1977 and 1980, there is a slight dip in the rate, with a sharp rise to 41 of every 1,000 African American in 1981. The rate falls in 1982 and bottoms out in 1986 with a low of

25 of every 1,000. It bounces sharply in 1987 and hovers between 30 and 35 of every 1,000 for the rest of the period.

Again, the increases and decline in the victimization rates are indicative of heightening levels of social distress in black communities. According to our theory of countervailing forces, distress should lead to less civic participation. In the aggregate, a decline in black people being victimized by crime would make African Americans feel safe to engage in civic and social activities without the fear of being victimized by crime.

CONCLUSION

Trends in the economic, social, and political conditions of African Americans show periods of progress and retrogression in the post–civil rights era. Clearly, advances have been made in the political life of African Americans. As blacks move farther away from the activist 1960s, more blacks have been elected to public office, a direct sign that political progress has been made since the civil rights movement. Additionally, blacks have become incorporated in the Democratic Party, where their policy preferences are represented – either substantively or symbolically – in Democratic presidential administrations. Recognition of blacks' enhanced empowerment since the civil rights movement would also be realized through the presidential election challenges of Jesse Jackson in 1984 and 1988. Hands that once picked cotton helped to energize the formidable Democratic presidential campaigns of Jesse Jackson. Additionally, the growing number of blacks attending colleges provides the potential for greater levels of empowerment because increases in social status should lead to greater levels of black participation in the polity.

The economic and social conditions of African-American life in the post–civil rights era have not been as bright. Rising levels of economic inequality among blacks may be leading to greater levels of political polarization among blacks. Periods of high unemployment, inflation, and immigration have presented economic setbacks for African Americans. And high levels of criminal victimization of blacks may have further eroded advances in blacks' quality of life in the United States.

In his 1980 "State of Black America Report," then Urban League President Vernon Jordan retrospectively looked back at the progress that African Americans had made in the first full decade since the civil rights movement. Arguing that blacks had lost ground but made some progress, Jordan notes that

> Not all the losses can be laid at the doorstep of "benign neglect" or its offspring "the new negativism," for certainly inflation and the general unfavorable economic conditions throughout the decade played their important roles as well. Nor did all blacks lose ground. For many, new job opportunities opened up, fresh educational opportunities developed, better housing and health care became available, and life was richly satisfying. Nor did all our allies turn to other interests. Many of them continued to believe in and work for equality of opportunity. But on balance, it is clear that with depression level unemployment and the majority of blacks on the lower rungs of the economic ladder at decade's end, the 70's were not the time of progress within Black America.
>
> (1980, iii)

We examine the impact of black political empowerment and macroeconomic and social forces on aggregate levels of black civic participation in the post–civil rights era. The ups and downs of the economic, social, and political fortunes will tell us how change in those fortunes affects the civic engagement of African Americans in this time span. But before we analyze the effects of those factors, in the next chapter we take a look at the theoretical and analytical justifications for analyzing changes in black participation through aggregate-level estimates rather than individual measures of black participation.

3

Studying Group Activism

Toward a Macro Approach to Black Civic Participation

I am because we are.

African proverb

We have now surveyed the economic, social, and political forces that characterize the political progress and the social and economic setbacks of African Americans in the post–civil rights era. Our theory of countervailing forces argues that political empowerment and social and economic distress have competing effects on black civic participation. In exploring the opposing forces of empowerment and distress, we take a macro approach to analyzing black civic and political participation. Rather than examining black civic participation as an artifact of individual behavior, we examine black participation in aggregates, which allows us to present a more analytically consistent profile of black civic activism than previous studies.

Consider the two fictional families we profiled in Chapter 1, the Jeffersons and the Evans. Each member from both families has different levels of participation. Louise Jefferson participates more than her husband George, but Louise and Florida Evans might participate at the same level, and both women might participate less than Florida's son, Michael. Even though George Jefferson's participation is lower than his wife's, it might be higher than James Evans' participation levels, whose participation might be lower than his daughter Thelma's, but only slightly lower than his son, J.J.'s. The participation of the

Jefferson's son Lionel might be less than that of his parents, and all the members of the Evans family. While estimating each person's participation level provides information about the Jeffersons and Evans as individual actors, only by aggregating the civic participation of each member of both families do we get an accurate portrayal of their activities as a reflection of group behavior. Thus in our study of black civic participation, we consider aggregate levels of participation as the unit of analysis to analyze black civic participation in the post–civil rights era. This approach provides an analytically consistent profile of black participation as group behavior. Before we provide our reasoning for aggregating black civic participation, we briefly review the current literature on black political behavior and demonstrate that our macro-level approach is beneficial for explaining fluctuations in aggregate levels of black civic participation since the modern civil rights movement.

The literature in black political behavior assumes that black political preferences and activities are group-based phenomena. But the theoretical level of analysis – that is, the explanation given for black political behavior – often does not match the empirical unit of analysis, which relies on the individual reports of African Americans that are supposed to reflect the behavior of the group. This disconnection between theory and evidence is reflected by a commitment to methodological individualism, a form of analysis that assumes that "all social phenomena – their structure and their change – are in principle explicable in ways that only involve individuals – their properties, their goals, their beliefs and their actions" (Elster 1987, 5). This commitment to methodological individualism is dominant in the study of American politics and is replicated in the study of African-American politics. However, because the theoretical underpinnings of African-American politics are largely about the study of blacks as a social group and not the individual behavior of black people, the commitment to methodological individualism in the study of black civic life has its limitations.

The disconnection between theory and evidence is reflected in some of the most important work on black civic behavior, too numerous to mention here (see, for example, Bobo and Gilliam 1990; Dawson 1994a; Tate 1994; Harris 1999a). These works often acknowledge the limitations of their data and try to work around those limitations by theorizing about the mechanisms that connect individual-level reports of behavior to the aggregate behavior of blacks as a group. Using individual levels of analysis derived from survey research, Michael Dawson, for example, argues that the homogeneity in black political preferences reflects the collective preferences of African Americans. In arguing for a linked-fate theory of black political life, in which blacks make judgments about their political preferences based on what is best for blacks as a group, Dawson tests "competing explanations of individual-level African-American politics" (1994a, 12). While Dawson's individualist approach highlights differences *within* the black population, which rightly reflect complexities in black political behavior, the approach, nonetheless, reduces group behavior to individual accounts.

Dawson's theory assumes the existence of collective behavior by appealing to psychology, economics, and history as a way to buttress his claims about group behavior in black political life. For instance, Dawson argues that psychology helps to illustrate the collective dynamics of black political life because it "describes how individuals process information and how groups influence individual cognition and behavior" (1994a, 12). Economic theories of rationality "offer clues about the decision-making process in which individuals engage once identity has been determined and preferences have been formed" but these micro processes reflect group behavior because they provide "insight into the decision-making processes of African-Americans as individuals and as part of a politically active group within the American polity" (1994a, 12). History also serves as a bridge between the individual and the group. The historical experiences of African Americans, and the indigenous institutions that evolved from the legacy of racial domination in the United States, shaped the "culture, norms, values, policy positions, and modes of behavior" of African Americans as a group (1994a, 13).

While the appropriation of psychological, economic, and historical perspectives provide a theoretically rich perspective on African-American politics, the empirical evidence is anchored in methodological individualism rather than what Jon Elster describes as methodological collectivism, an approach that specifically considers "supra-individual entities" that are important explanatory forces in human behavior (Elster 1987, 6). Without a methodological collectivist approach, an analytical leap is made about the collective political behavior of blacks based on individual assessments rather than aggregated behavior that would reflect the actions and beliefs of blacks as a group. To put it another way, micro-level evidence is used to make claims about macro-level behavior.

This mismatch between theory, evidence, and inference in the study of black political behavior has been raised by Hanes Walton (1985). In a critique of the behaviorist approach in political science generally and in African-American politics in particular, Walton argues in his book *Invisible Politics* that political behaviorism, and the discipline of political science writ large, emphasizes individual behavior over the behavior of collectives. Walton's critiques are important because they highlight the methodological problems that arise when analyzing black political behavior through the behavior of blacks as individuals rather than as a group. Walton asks how claims about black political behavior – a behavior that assumes group-based attributes – can be made when the unit of analysis for that behavior is the individual rather than the collective.

To Walton, the emphasis on individualism is not only a methodological flaw in the study of black life but also has normative implications for how black political behavior is interpreted. As Walton observes, the "individual-centered behavioral approach in black political behavior has produced a vast literature that proposes the individual weaknesses and imperfections it undercovers are a result of blacks' individual shortcomings and not the result of any systematic factors under which they have labored" (1985, 3). Thus, explanations of black political behavior are often attributed to the individual shortcomings of blacks, such as apathy, low educational achievement, or low levels of political efficacy or trust. These shortcomings have been used to explain, for instance, persistent lower levels in the civic participation of blacks when compared to whites.

Not only does the commitment to methodological individualism raise questions about the need to consider political context when analyzing black civic behavior, but Walton's critique also highlights the need to consider macro-level factors as forces that either constrain or enhance the civic behavior of blacks as a group. Walton notes, for example, that the focus on the individual in black political behavior "implies that institutional arrangements, structural devices, organizational types and legal rules do not affect political behavior as much as intrapsychic and sociopsychological forces do" (Walton 1985, 3).

Thus, by moving from the individual, micro-level unit of analysis to a collective, macro-level unit of analysis, our macro approach to black civic participation provides a more coherent portrait of black civic activism as a group phenomenon and allows us to determine specifically how exogenous political and structural forces (such as levels of black political empowerment and social and economic distress) might bear upon aggregate-level fluctuations in black civic involvement over time.

In taking a macro approach to black civic participation, we move beyond methodological individualism and time-bound constraints by considering aggregate levels of black civic activity as a proxy for group activism and analyzing changes in collective behavior over time. In the first part of this chapter, we discuss the shortcomings of past empirical research on black civic behavior and demonstrate how our alternative macro-level approach is better suited for explaining the dynamics of black civic activism in the post–civil rights era. We now proceed by building upon our critiques of black political behavior as a reflection of individual assessments by demonstrating that black civic participation as group behavior can be operationalized and measured using simple statistical reasoning principles. In addition, we track our new aggregate-level measures of participation over a twenty-one-year period from 1973 to 1994, thinking carefully about how various structural factors might account for ebbs and flows in black civic engagement. Before we accomplish these tasks, however, we need to provide an analytical argument about why it is important to consider aggregate levels of black civic activity over individual assessments of civic behavior.

THEORY, EVIDENCE, AND INFERENCES IN THE STUDY OF BLACK PARTICIPATION

In order to empirically study and make inferences about black civic life as group behavior, analysts' research designs and interpretation strategies must be consistent. Specifically, each of these elements must be logically connected at a similar stratum to produce an accurate account of black civic participation. Figures 3.1 and 3.2 depict two distinct analytic approaches. Figure 3.1 characterizes the analytic approach dominant in the study of black civic life. As the diagram shows, past

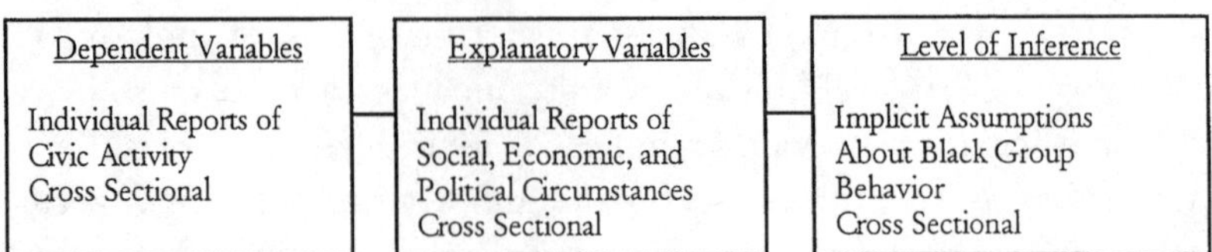

FIGURE 3.1. Research strategy with mixed data and levels of inference.

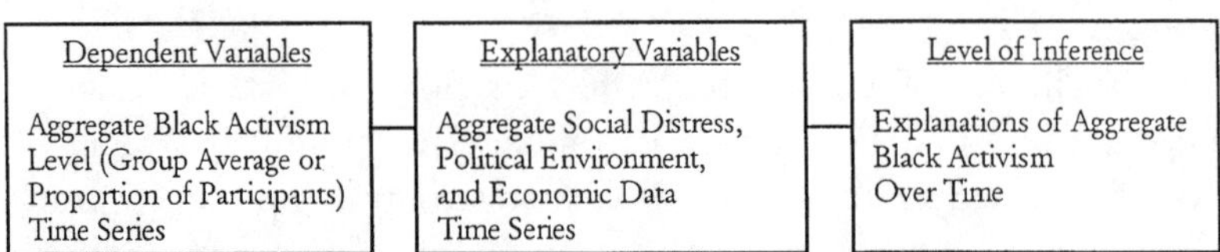

FIGURE 3.2. Research strategy with similar data and levels of inference.

studies have typically utilized individual-level survey data regarding respondents' social, economic, and political status as explanatory variables for understanding black civic participation (Bobo and Gilliam 1990; Tate 1991; Cohen and Dawson 1993; Tate 1994). Even though these works often acknowledge the limitations of cross-sectional survey data, the authors' inferences and conclusions implicitly purport to explain the participation of blacks as a group. However, individual reports of civic activity *alone* are ill suited to provide an insight into the civic participation of blacks as a group. A coherent account about how individual involvement translates at the group level must accompany analyses of African-American civic behavior.

In contrast to the individual as the unit of analysis, Figure 3.2 permits us to make reliable inferences about black group participation by utilizing a macro-level approach. Our strategy employs both aggregate-level measures of black civic participation as well as macro-level explanatory variables. A solution to the problems of past research is gained by matching theory, measures, and inferences of black behavior. It is essential to note that this strategy does not cross levels of inference and create data interpretation difficulties. In particular, we do not incur problems associated with ecological fallacies because we are not attempting to recover, understand, and make claims about individual black behavior using aggregate data. Rather, we use *aggregate*-level political, economic, and social distress indicators to explain changes in *aggregate* levels of black civic participation over time.

FROM INDIVIDUAL TO COLLECTIVE PROPERTIES

We should note that macro-level explanations of political phenomena have been considered in other areas of American politics. A number of scholars have studied the collective dimensions of American public opinion and its response to changes in the political and economic environment (MacKuen, Erikson, and Stimson 1989; Page and Shapiro 1992; Erikson et al. 2002). In addition, macro-level political studies have also investigated the impact of national economic conditions on aggregate voting behavior (Kramer 1971; Arcelus and Meltzer 1975; Kramer 1983; Markus 1988). These studies highlight the importance of distinguishing between individual and collective accounts of political behavior.

MacKuen, Erikson, and Stimson, for instance, introduced the idea of systematically analyzing changes in aggregate partisanship and its consequences for American political behavior. In their study, macro partisanship is measured as the percentages of party identifiers who support Democrats (1989, 1128). The authors show that, contrary to individual partisanship stability, aggregate levels of partisanship fluctuated from 1945 to 1987 and that a one-point shift in partisanship yields a three-seat gain in House elections (1989, 1129). In addition, MacKuen and colleagues demonstrate that macroeconomic and political forces affect partisan divisions in the electorate.

In their more recent work *The Macro Polity*, Erikson, MacKuen, and Stimson build upon their earlier research on macro political behavior by providing "a sustained examination of American politics from the aggregate persective" (2002, xxi). In this work, the authors show how citizens' collective responses to the economy make sense in light of their aggregate perceptions of economic events. Moreover, they argue that aggregate-level partisanship responds to various social and political events that citizens experience in their daily lives. In addition, they find that the collective ideological mood of the nation changes with the ebbs and flows of the political and economic environment. Finally, this team of researchers argues that election outcomes are influenced by the electorates' collective partisanship leanings and the nation's general ideological mood. Based on all of this evidence, the authors conclude, "while individuals may appear uniformed and inattentive to politics at the micro level, as a collective they are, nonetheless, competent and prudent representatives and governmental institutions respond to their political needs and desires" (2002, 447). Together, the earlier and more recent studies provide ample evidence that generalizations about individual attitudes do not hold at the aggregate level and citizens' perceptions of macro-level political and economic forces influence aggregate-level political outcomes (Erikson et al. 2002, xxi).

Page and Shapiro's (1992) work also draws attention to the dissimilarity between individual and collective political attitudes. The authors maintain that unlike cross-sectional, individual opinion reports, "the collective policy preferences of the American public are predominantly rational, generally stable, and form coherent and mutually consistent patterns that make sense in terms of underlying values and available information." Page and Shapiro (1992, xi) argue that changes in the collective policy preferences of citizens respond to international events and social and economic changes reported in the media. Moreover, their study is invaluable to our understanding of macro-level behavior because it illustrates how statistical aggregation processes transform unstable, individual reports of political attitudes into coherent aggregate reflections of collective opinion. In answering the question, "why aggregate preferences," they contend

> the answer has to do with the statistical aggregation process, in which the expressed opinions of many individuals are summed or combined into a collective whole, and with social processes in which many people receive communications and think and talk with each other. These processes give collective public opinion and collective survey responses certain "emergent" properties that are not shared by the individual opinions and responses that make them up. (1992, 14–15)

As any observer of black political life might suspect, these aggregation processes are also important for understanding black civic participation. In particular, African Americans regularly interact in various social and political settings, exchanging information about events and issues that are relevant to black communities. This interdependence often changes the quantities of civic participation for blacks as a group.[1] Consequently, aggregate levels of black activism are a function

[1] Here our argument is similar to Schelling's (1978, 13–14), Page and Shapiro's (1992, 14–15), and Erikson, MacKuen, and Stimson's (2002, 10–11) notions about how individual-level interactions between citizens influence the characteristics of group-level political behavior and attitudes.

of both individual considerations and racial group concerns stimulated by interaction in black social contexts. These communal dimensions of African-American civic engagement have not been properly considered and operationalized in previous research efforts. To address this concern, we propose a macro-level approach to black civic participation.

BEYOND METHODOLOGICAL INDIVIDUALISM AND TIME-BOUND ANALYSES

Our macro theory of black civic participation makes the claim that aggregate levels of black civic involvement provide a more holistic depiction of black civic activity as group behavior than individual accounts of black participation. We provide two explanations for this claim. The first is the role that social interaction plays in enhancing civic participation beyond the individual and the second explanation involves the role of what we describe as "black political entrepreneurs." We define black political entrepreneurs as organizations and movements that primarily seek and target blacks to support their political aims and goals.

Figure 3.3 illustrates how varying contexts of social interaction among blacks produce different sets of interpretations about the collective civic participation of African Americans. Social interaction among blacks is an important element of our civic participation model because it allows aggregate levels of black participation to exceed the sum of its individual components. This interaction is sustained by indigenous organizations and institutions (such as churches, civic organizations, and educational institutions) and social norms that promote group solidarity (the feelings of linked fate with other blacks, the commitment to same-race relationships, or the belief in social distance from whites). We argue that the existence of indigenous institutions and social norms of solidarity among blacks produces higher levels of civic engagement for blacks as a group than would be expected if blacks were not socially interacting.

The first circle in Figure 3.3 illustrates black civic participation in a universe where no social interaction with other blacks occurs. In this universe, there are also no institutions or organizations that are indigenous to the black population nor are there norms of group solidarity, two factors that would enhance the civic engagement of blacks as a group. Although this is an unrealistic portrayal of social dynamics in

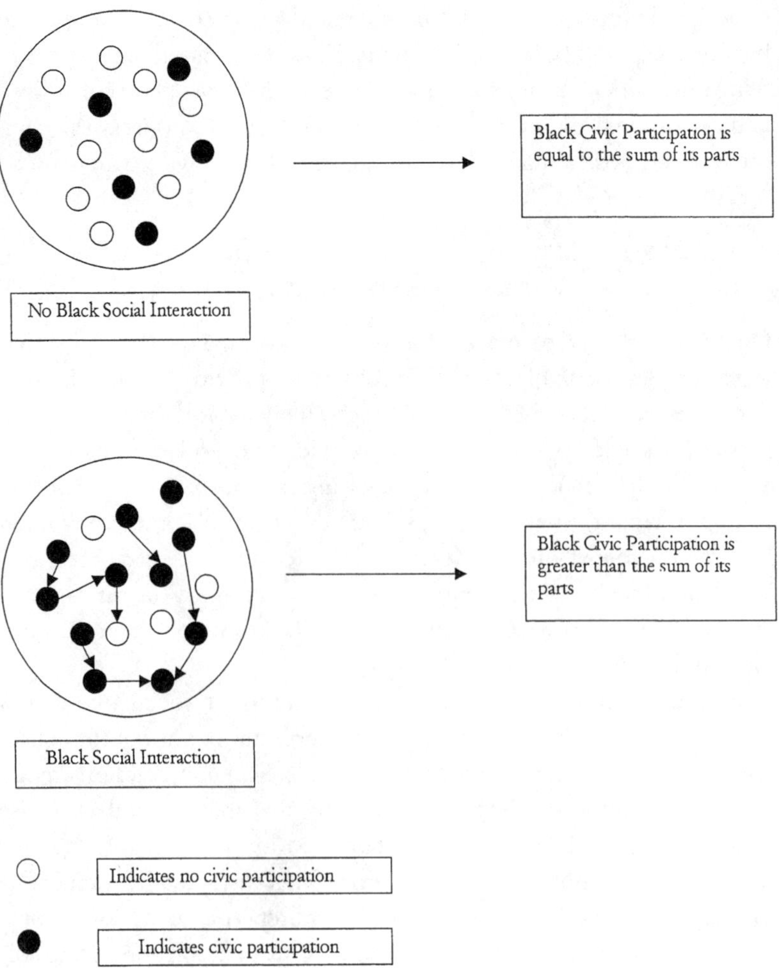

FIGURE 3.3. Social interaction and aggregation in black civic participation.

black communities, analyses based on individual rather than aggregated reports of civic participation cannot account for processes that enhance the civic involvement of blacks as a group. Thus, with no social interaction, aggregate levels of black participation would be equal to the sum of its parts, meaning that the group-based dynamics that are generated through social interactions in the black population are not accounted for in the analysis of individual reports of black civic participation.

In contrast, the second circle in Figure 3.3, illustrates black civic participation in a universe where social interaction takes place among blacks. In this scenario, interaction enhances the aggregate-level participation of blacks above what would be expected if there was no interaction among blacks. As Thomas Schelling observes about contingent behavior – that is, the idea that one's behavior is contingent on what others are doing – individuals are influenced by the actions of individuals in their social environment. Here, contingent behavior depends on the "system of interaction between individuals and their environment, that is between individuals and other individuals or between individuals and the collectivity" (1978, 14).

As the second circle demonstrates, there are chains of social interaction in the universe of the black population that enhance the civic participation levels in the population. In this universe, there are blacks who participate in civic activities without socially interacting with other blacks, and there are blacks who do not participate despite their social interaction with other blacks. There are also blacks who are neither active in American civic life nor socially connected with other blacks. However, despite different levels of social interaction within the population, the civic participation of the group is greater than what would be expected if there were no interaction among blacks. Hence, where black participation is contingent on some degree of social interaction among some individual blacks but not all blacks, the black population produces a level of participation that is greater than the sum of its parts.

We do not make the claim that social interaction is static. We are mindful that the degree of social interaction may increase or decrease over time as will the strength of indigenous institutions and norms of solidarity that sustain social interaction (Dawson 1994b). For example, during the era of legalized segregation when indigenous institutions and norms of solidarity were stronger than they are today, social interactions among blacks were vibrant, though the opportunities to participate were constrained in the context of Jim Crow. But when opportunities for black opposition to segregation expanded, those interactions facilitated black mobilization during the civil rights movement (McAdam 1982; Morris 1984). In the post–segregation era, when institutions and norms of solidarity are weakening, social interaction among blacks is becoming less dynamic, which might consequently lower the participation level of blacks as a group. However, despite changes in social interaction among blacks over time, we contend that social interactions still produce levels of black participation that are greater than what would occur if there were no social interaction in the black population.

The mechanism of social interaction is only part of the story of why the sum of individual black civic participation is greater than its party. Social interaction has to work with some other process to ground our explanation for aggregation since, in theory, noninteraction among blacks can produce the same results as a socially interactive black population if blacks are socially interacting with individuals who are not black. If, in the first circle, those engaged in civic activities are socially connected with individuals outside the circle, then their participation can also be socially contingent, thereby enhancing the civic activism of blacks as a group in absence of any interaction among blacks.

It is here that black political entrepreneurs are an important link between social interaction and aggregation processes in black civic participation. Again, we define black political entrepreneurs as any political group or movement, from the National Association for the Advancement of Colored People (NAACP) to the Nation of Islam, that is dependent on black constituencies for its viability. These entrepreneurs use their resources to mobilize blacks in support of a movement or organization's goals. As strategic actors in pursuit of goals, it is more efficient for entrepreneurs to initiate political activities among blacks in a universe where blacks are socially interacting than in one where there is no interaction among blacks. Thus, these entrepreneurs enhance the civic participation of blacks as a group by directly and indirectly mobilizing blacks who are socially connected. For example, a group of blacks may be asked to write a letter about police brutality to their congressional representative by an NAACP official who speaks during a black church service. Or, a member of the Nation of Islam may appeal to patrons of a neighborhood barber shop to attend a rally on police brutality. Through political entrepreneurs who seek support from blacks through social interaction in the black population, the civic participation of blacks as a group is enhanced beyond what we would expect in a world where blacks are not socially interacting with other blacks. Thus, aggregate-level accounts of black civic participation are a more accurate interpretation of black civic activism as group behavior than individual reports.

A THEORY OF COLLECTIVE PARTICIPATION, NOT COLLECTIVE PREFERENCES

Our macro-centered perspective on black civic activism does not directly consider the preferences and attitudes of blacks as a determinant of black civic participation. We assume that preferences, like collective participation, are not static but vary across time. In any given moment, individual blacks or segments in the black population are motivated to participate in a variety of activities that are linked to particular issues or ideological commitments. The ideological motivations for those activities can sway between black nationalism, feminism, class-centered ideologies, or even American patriotism, among other preferences. We make no claims of what Adolph Reed describes as a "corporate black interest," the idea that blacks share similar group interests and that those interests influence the political participation of blacks as a group (1999). Rather, our aim is to explore how aggregate levels of black civic participation differ from their individual-level components and demonstrate how macro levels of black civic involvement change over time. We are also interested in explaining how various macro-level political, economic, and social distress forces may influence aggregate-level movements in black civic participation. Later, we say more about how these forces either depress or stimulate changes in black civic engagement. We now consider the statistical representation of aggregated-levels of black civic participation.

THE STATISTICAL LOGIC OF MACRO-LEVEL PARTICIPATION

To empirically capture macro levels of black civic activism, we rely on simple statistical reasoning principles. Drawing on Page and Shapiro's (1992, 19–23) logic of aggregation, we demonstrate how the civic participation of individual black citizens can be meaningfully amassed into a distinct social collective. The aggregation strategy and method we use

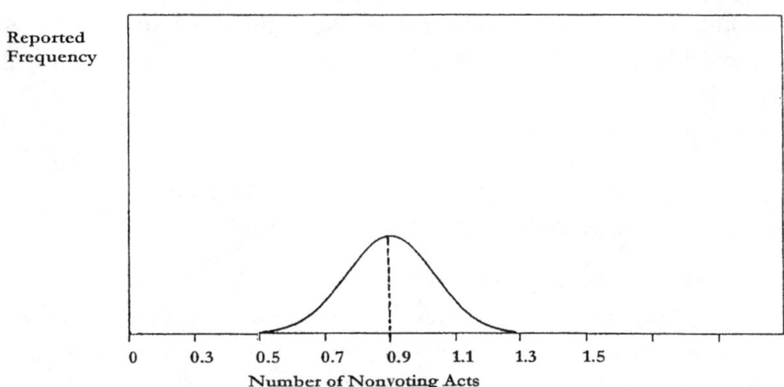

FIGURE 3.4. Hypothetical distribution of a black individual's participation level over time.

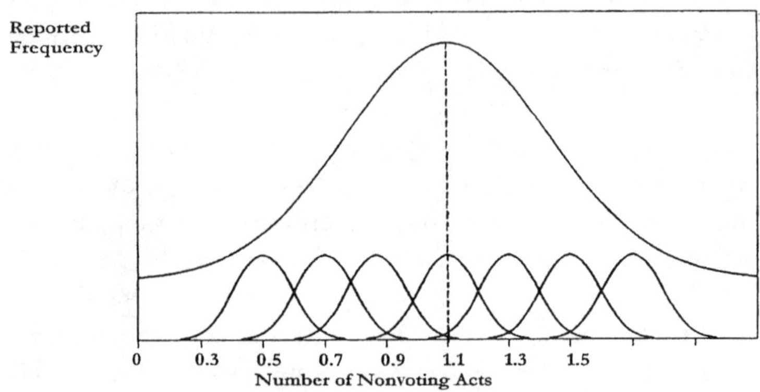

FIGURE 3.5. Hypothetical distribution of an aggregate black civic participation over time (Adapted from Page and Shapiro 1992).

considers the mobilizing capacity of black social networks and political entrepreneurs and incorporates their overall influence on group civic activism. We discuss the logic of black macro participation in Figures 3.4 and 3.5. These figures illustrate how the participatory activity of black individuals combines to form a collective distribution of African-American civic involvement.

In Figure 3.4, we assume that each individual has a long-term distribution of civic activism that can be approximated by a normal distribution.[2] In this diagram, the horizontal axis measures the number of civic acts an individual engages in, and the vertical axis depicts the number of responses an individual provided. At various moments in a person's life, one may report involvement in zero, one, or more forms of activity. However, over time an individual's "true" level of activism will be reflected as the central tendency of this distribution (vertical dashed line). At the micro level, this average quantity of participation is influenced by individual-level factors such as strength of partisanship, socioeconomic factors, individual perceptions of the political environment for blacks, and the political information black citizens receive and process in their daily lives. Understanding how these explanatory factors shape the individual tendencies and contours of activism preoccupies a substantial portion of black civic participation research. However, when we shift attention to investigating the aggregate levels of civic engagement in the entire black population, we must employ a statistical reasoning strategy that sums these individual participatory tendencies into a meaningful aggregate.

Figure 3.6 graphically demonstrates how single participation distributions for many individuals can be amalgamated into macro levels of black participation. In this diagram, the central tendency of the larger, elevated macro distribution curve (vertical dashed line) represents the average participation level of all the smaller individual distributions. This collective central tendency of black activism can be operationalized using a numerical average of black participatory acts or a proportional frequency in which most individuals engaged in a particular civic act (see Page and Shapiro 1992, 16–17). In terms of statistical properties, this new macro entity reflects the micro activism tendencies of black individuals and accounts for social interaction effects among African Americans to produce a meaningful composite of black

[2] We use this normality assumption as a convenience for explanation purposes. We are aware that some black citizens' participatory behavior cannot be characterized in such a symmetric fashion. Often individuals' activism distributions will be less symmetric and better approximated by other distributions. Nonetheless, in these cases, the alternative distributions will also have derivable central tendencies upon which the general logic of our argument will still apply. Our basic point is that an approximately normal distribution of responses around a central tendency would occur for the collective when the responses are aggregated (see Page and Shapiro 1992, 19–23, 28).

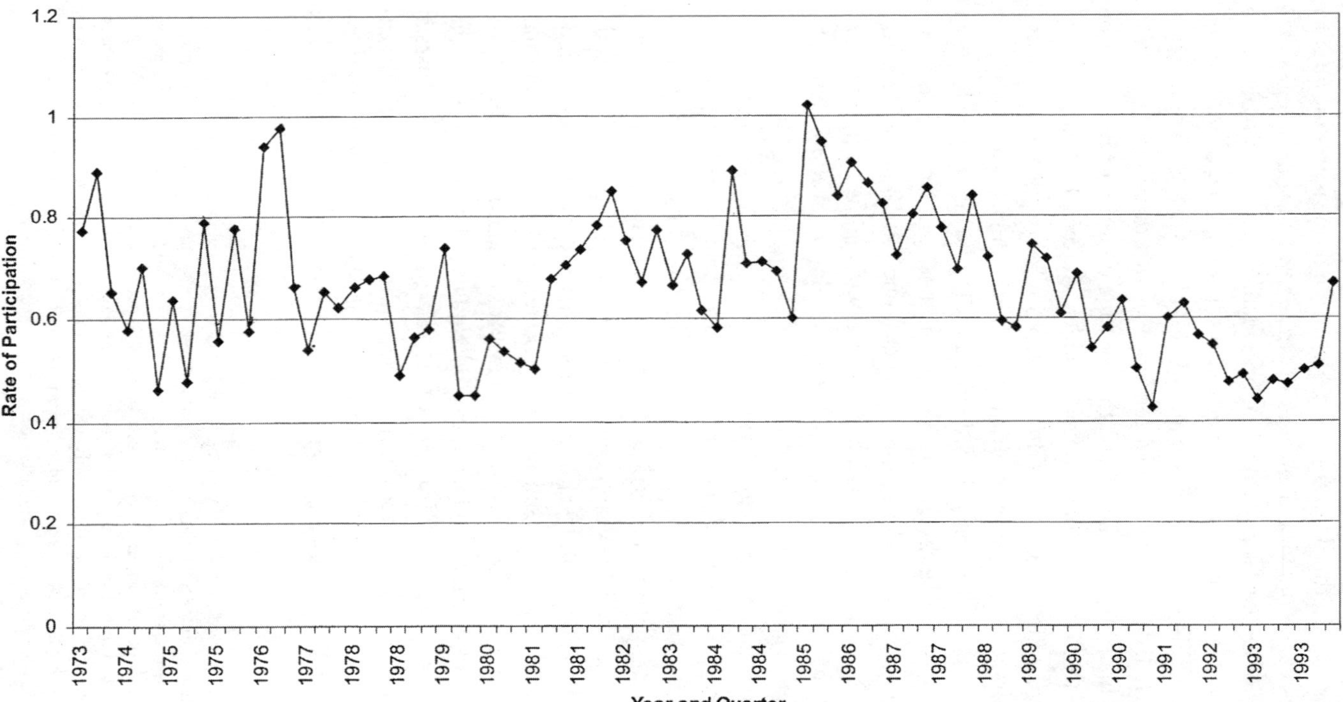

FIGURE 3.6. Composite political participation index, 1973–1994.

participation as group behavior. This pooled quantity is an appropriate measure of group-level activism and will be used to make inferences about collective black civic involvement.

DATA AND MEASURES

Building upon our theoretical and statistical logic, we employ nationally representative survey data on African Americans to explore further the dimensions of black civic participation. Our analyses utilize black respondents from the Roper Social and Political Trends data set, a collection of survey questions on civic participation that was asked on a quarterly basis from 1973 to 1994. The Roper data set does not include questions about respondents' voting behavior. Again, we focus our analyses on examining blacks' nonvoting, civic participation. In addition, our interest in nonelectoral forms of black civic activism is motivated by the dearth of literature on this topic, in comparison to many studies of black voting behavior (see, for example, Tate 1991; Tate 1994).

We consider twelve modes of civic participation in our analysis. Respondents were asked if they had participated in any of the following acts in the *previous twelve months*: (1) wrote to a congressperson or senator, (2) attended a political rally or speech, (3) attended a public meeting on town or school affairs, (4) held or ran for office, (5) served on a committee for some local organization, (6) became or served as an officer for an organization, (7) wrote a letter to a paper, (8) signed a petition, (9) worked for a political party, (10) made a speech, (11) wrote an article for a magazine or newspaper, or (12) joined a group interested in better government. Based on our macro participation argument, we combine these modes of participation into three indices of black civic involvement (1) a composite black civic participation index, (2) a black political work index, and (3) a black organizational participation index.[3]

Using the Roper survey responses about citizen's participation in these twelve civic activities, we construct two indices of civic activity

[3] We replicate the scales used by Burns, Schlozman, and Verba (2001, 69) in their study of gender differences in political participation to construct our three indices of civic participation.

examining political work and organizational work, respectively. Our *Political Work Index* is an additive index of the following activities: attending a rally or speech, being an active member in a political party, membership in a political organization such as the NAACP, and signing a petition. The *Organizational Work Index* is an additive index of the following: serving as an officer for an organization, service on a committee for a local organization, making a speech, and attending a public meeting on town or school affairs. We also employ a third measure, the *Composite Participation Index*, which includes all of the twelve civic participation items we previously mentioned. All of these dependent variables are quarterly averages in each period between 1973 and 1994 (for descriptives, see Appendices A and B). These participation indices also reflect the long-term tendencies of aggregate-level activism for blacks as a group and allow us to paint a picture of how levels of African-American civic involvement expand or contract over time.

DETERMINANTS OF AGGREGATE POLITICAL BEHAVIOR IN PAST STUDIES

Most aggregate-level electoral behavior studies examine the impact of macroeconomic variables on aggregate election outcomes (for a review see Kramer 1971). Although the results were mixed, scholars typically agree that macroeconomic conditions such as inflation and income levels affect election results, with economic upturns helping the incumbent party candidates and economic problems benefiting the opposition (Kramer 1971, 140–1). Nevertheless, aggregate election outcomes are not the only relevant consideration for understanding macro-level civic and political behavior.

Increasing our current knowledge about citizens' collective level of civic engagement is also beneficial. In particular, Arcelus and Meltzer (1975, 1232) suggest that changes in the participation rates of voters often are larger than changes in the share of votes received by the major parties. Thus, because aggregate participation rates are subject to variability, it seems prudent to understand what factors influence these changes. As we noted earlier, we believe that aggregate-level black participation in running election campaigns, attending protest demonstrations, signing petitions, contacting public officials, and making campaign contributions is influenced by shifting macro-level economic, social, and political forces. However, to date, few scholars have directly examined the effects of national economic and social distress indicators on various aggregate-level measures of black civic participation.[4] We briefly review this related literature.

MACRO FORCES AND PARTICIPATION

Arcelus and Meltzer analyze the impact of national economic indicators on aggregate levels of political participation for the entire American electorate. They contend that, with the exception of inflation, aggregate economic variables did not affect the percentage of eligible voters participating in congressional elections from 1896 to 1970. Specifically, they argue that "high rates of inflation lower the participation rate, but the reduction is not significant" (1975, 1238).[5] Even though they find that inflation does not have a substantial effect on voting turnout, their study helps us to think about how macro-level structural forces might adversely influence black civic involvement. Consequently, we build upon this work by explicitly considering how changing macroeconomic conditions (such as rising price levels) and shifting social and political environments (such as increasing income disparities among blacks and greater numbers of black elected officials) might affect aggregate levels of black civic participation in the post–civil rights era.

Another study that directly relates to our research on aggregate-level black civic activism is Matthews and Prothro's *Negroes and the New*

[4] Previous aggregated studies of black participation only employ regional or local-level aggregate economic and social indicators. For example, Fenton and Vines's (1957) study of Negro registration utilized census reports and data from local sources on economic tenancy and urbanicity characteristics. The aggregation level of these explanatory factors was the state or parish. In addition, Matthews and Prothro (1966, 101–73) examined the effects of *county-level* social, economic, and political variables on aggregate, southern Negro political participation. However, the authors were primarily interested in describing the politics of southern communities.

[5] Goodman and Kramer (1975) raised serious research design and methodological questions about Arcelus and Meltzer's findings, ultimately arguing that the authors' inferences about the effects of economic conditions on election outcomes were not supported by the evidence presented. However, their critique did not focus on Arcelus and Meltzer's findings about aggregate participation rates.

Southern Politics. In their classic work, Matthews and Prothro studied the effects of county-level social, economic, and political variables on aggregate, southern black political participation. Their research is pertinent to our analysis because they carefully analyze the relationship between aggregate-level explanatory factors and aggregate black political participation rates. They discovered that even though individual attributes are important for explaining black political involvement, their importance was circumscribed or facilitated by the general characteristics of the counties where individuals lived (1966, 133). Thus, their findings suggest that a strictly individual-level approach to black civic behavior is problematic for understanding the complexities of African-American civic participation. Clearly, macro-level structural forces also shape black civic engagement. In addition, we should also note that while Matthews and Prothro explicitly focused on aggregate-level black political participation, the cumulative levels of their explanatory variables are southern counties, rather than the United States as a whole. Moreover, their findings are based on southern county data that was collected in the early 1960s. Consequently, the substantial social and political changes that have taken place since the civil rights movement require us to ask questions about more contemporary factors that might influence black civic activism.

In sum, most studies of black civic participation rely on individual-level data from regional or nationally representative surveys (Matthews and Prothro 1966; Miller et al. 1981; Shingles 1981; Bobo and Gilliam 1990; Tate 1991; Cohen and Dawson 1993; Tate 1994). Moreover, the macro political behavior research literature often exclusively focuses on whites in the general population and neglects the unique political experience of African Americans. In addition, the reliability of previous aggregate-level studies is hindered by their historical examination of southern civic and political behavior (Price 1955; Ladd 1966, 7–47; Matthews and Prothro 1966) and their use of only basic summary statistics on black civic participation (Price 1955; Ladd 1966, 17–47; Conway 2000, 33). We improve upon these limitations by developing a coherent macro-level, theoretical, and empirical account of black civic participation in the post–civil rights era. Furthermore, we use national survey data to create a variety of aggregate-level measures of black civic activities and track their movements from 1973 to 1994.

EXPECTATIONS OF OUR MACRO MODEL OF BLACK PARTICIPATION

The findings from previous aggregate-level studies of political behavior (especially Erikson et al. 2002) provide us with some general guidelines regarding the macro dynamics of our participation model. To clarify our black civic participation argument, we formally state the assumptions and expectations of our macro approach. We contend that

- Aggregate levels of black civic activism are generally stable in the post–civil rights era.
- However, despite the stability in aggregate black civic activism, fluctuations in activism are influenced by aggregate changes in the political, social, and economic environments.
- These patterns reflect the influence of macro-level explanatory factors that have an impact on the distribution of aggregate levels of black civic activism.
- Rather than focusing on the civic behavior of black individuals, scholars should direct their attention to the aggregate levels of activism for the entire group and its response to changes in the social, political, and economic environments.

In the next section of this chapter and later in Chapter 5, we empirically test and explore each of these claims using the Roper Social and Political Trends data. In particular, we pay close attention to how well the data supports our macro approach to black civic participation. Finally, we discuss how our macro approach allows us to better understand the dynamics of black civic engagement over time by highlighting the countervailing effects of adverse economic and social conditions for African Americans in an era of increasing black political empowerment.

TRENDS IN AGGREGATE LEVELS OF BLACK CIVIC PARTICIPATION

One way to test the expectations of our macro model of black civic participation is to examine trends in aggregate levels of black civic activism over time. Figure 3.6 reports the composite rates of civic participation for blacks from 1973 to 1994. One obvious finding from the Roper Trend data is that like most people in the general population most black Americans do not engage in civic activities (see Chapter 5 for comparisons among blacks, whites, and the general population). For example, in this twenty-one-year period, the average level of black civic participation ranges between 0.4 and 1.0 civic acts. In addition, the trend data shows that most of the participation data points in this series were in the 0.4 to 0.8 acts range. Moreover, our composite measure of black civic participation only approaches one civic act in late 1976 and exceeds one act in 1985.

We also see considerable volatility in black rates of civic participation during the post–civil rights era. From 1973 to 1975, black participation rates both increased and decreased at various points. In addition, from 1975 to 1976 black participation levels continued to fluctuate up and down, yet show a trend of rising levels of activism during this interval. Next, aggregate levels of black civic activism declined between 1976 and 1977. The 1977 to 1979 period is also marked by surges and declines in black civic engagement with a general increase in black civic involvement from 1978 to 1979. Thereafter, black participation levels drop between 1979 and 1980 and then steadily increase between 1980 to 1982. From 1982 to 1984, we see that black participation generally diminishes and then spikes in mid-1984. The story from 1984 to 1985 differs. Throughout this period, black participation declines and then takes a sharp upward turn by the end of 1985. After 1985, aggregate levels of black civic involvement continue to ebb and flow but consistently decline until 1991. By the end of 1991, black participation levels rise again and then decline throughout 1992. Finally, in 1993, black civic activism levels recover and continue to rise for the rest of the period.

Now we turn our attention to examining movement trends in the black political work index. Again, our index is measured by the following activities: attending a rally or speech, being a member of a political party, being a member of a political organization, and signing a petition. Figure 3.7 shows that aggregate levels of black political work activity have greatly fluctuated since the early 1970s. In 1973, black political work levels briefly increase and then decline for the next two years. From 1975 to 1977, blacks' aggregate-level participation in political work activities decreases and increases at various points, but generally rises in this time span. Next, the trend reverses and political work activities decrease between 1977 and 1978.

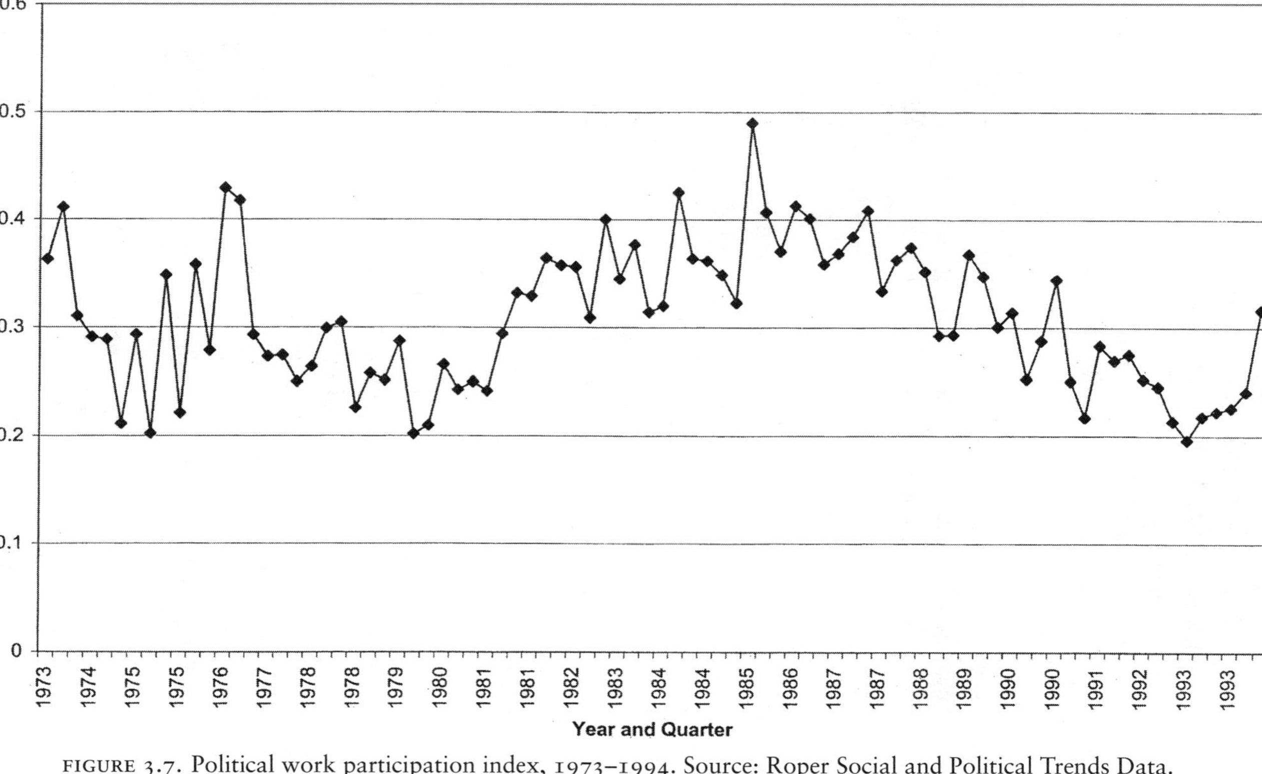

FIGURE 3.7. Political work participation index, 1973–1994. Source: Roper Social and Political Trends Data.

Volatility also characterizes aggregate black participation levels from 1978 to 1981. During this period, blacks' involvement in political work activities rises and falls in a tumultuous manner. From 1981 to 1983, we see that aggregate participation levels steadily increase with the exception of a slight decrease in black activism at the end of 1982. By 1983, aggregate black political work levels begin to fluctuate again until the end of 1984; it then descends throughout most of 1985. We also see that aggregate black political work levels spike during the first part of 1986 (the highest level in the series), rise and fall through 1993, but generally trend downward between 1986 and 1993. After 1993, blacks' participation levels continue to rise in a fairly consistent pattern.

Our black organizational participation measure tells a slightly different story about black civic activism. Recall that this index is a measure of organizational participation captured by serving as an officer for an organization, serving on a committee for a local organization, making a speech, and attending a public meeting on town or school affairs. Compared to the other indices, blacks' involvement in organizational modes of civic activity seems to be more variable over time. Based on Figure 3.8, it is clear that aggregate levels of black organizational participation ebb and flow in a more sporadic pattern than the other forms of civic involvement. Specifically, black organizational participation rises at the end of 1973 and then declines until 1974. From 1974 to 1976, black organizational participation rises and declines in an up-and-down pattern. By early 1977, black organizational participation reaches it peak (0.46 acts) and then declines in mid-1977. Afterward, organizational participation levels increase between 1977 and 1978, fall at the end of 1978, and then rise again by early 1979. From 1979 to 1980, black participation rates steeply decline and then dramatically rise from early 1980 to 1981. The two years between 1982 and 1984 show another decline in participation, followed by two spikes in black organizational involvement in early 1984 and late 1985. After 1985, we again witness many rises and declines in the level of participation, with a familiar overall trend of declining activism after 1986.

These wildly fluctuating patterns suggest that black organizational participation is a unique form of civic engagement compared to our other measures. It is likely that most African Americans rarely engage in these forms of organizational activism (such as serving as an officer

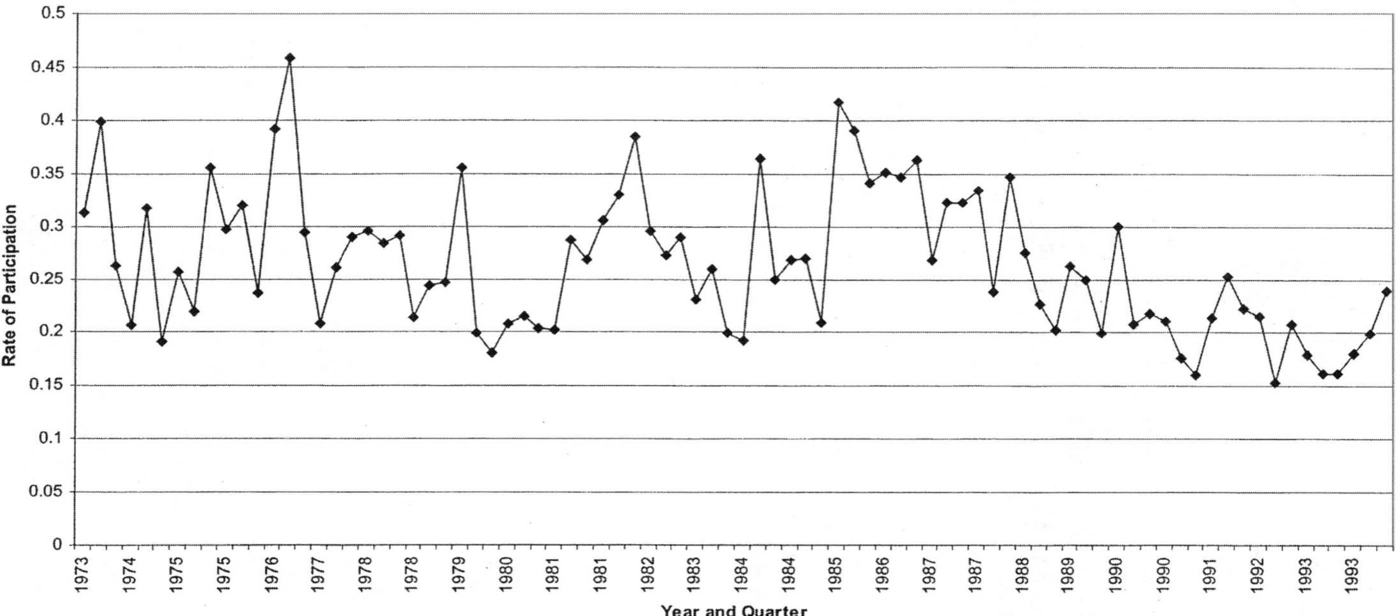

FIGURE 3.8. Organizational work participation index, 1973–1994.

for an organization, serving on a committee, and making a speech to a group), and this accounts for the greater levels of variability we observe in the black organizational participation series as compared to our index of political work. We also believe that these distinctions help to explain some of the findings we observe later in our multivariate analyses.

In sum, these trends demonstrate that black Americans' civic participation levels have been generally stable in the post–civil rights era, yet have fluctuated at particular moments in time. Although some levels of black group participation occur in a similar range, we also see that there are substantial fluctuations in the general patterns of black civic activism as we move forward in time from 1973 to 1994. As we noted earlier, aggregate levels of black civic involvement are subject to rise or fall at any given moment depending on the social, political, and economic conditions that blacks are experiencing at particular moments in time. Thus, we have evidence that supports the first expectation of our macro approach to black civic participation and some good indications that our second and third arguments (regarding ebbs and flows in activism) are also true. But what accounts for these movements and shifts in aggregate levels of black civic activism? We contend that our macro approach to black participation and its countervailing forces argument offers a compelling explanation for these changing levels of black civic engagement between 1973 and 1994. Looking ahead, in Chapter 5, we more carefully examine our second and third expectations regarding the causes of movements in black civic participation over time.

SUMMARY AND CONCLUSIONS

In this chapter, we set out to demonstrate the limitations of methodological individualism for the study of black group civic behavior. We then offered an alternative approach for explicitly theorizing and modeling macro-level black civic participation. Drawing from a handful of studies of macro behavior directly and indirectly related to black civic activism, we contend that social interaction between blacks and the behavior of black political entrepreneurs enhances the civic involvement of blacks as a group. This enhancement in group participation is not accounted for when only analyzing individual reports of black civic participation. Thus, by aggregating individual reports of civic activities into an aggregate profile of black civic engagement, a theoretically and empirically sound depiction of black activism emerges.

We also use our new aggregate-level measures of black civic participation to examine changes in black civic activism over time. The trend analysis that we present in this chapter is one of the first studies to plot and track movements in black civic behavior over a substantial period of time. As we mentioned earlier, the limitations of previous data on black civic behavior prevents scholars from understanding the dynamic properties of black civic participation. By using the Roper Trend data, however, we are able to show how each of our macro-level indicators of black civic activism (the composite black political participation index, the black political work participation index, and the black organizational work participation index) vary through out the post–civil rights era. We argue that these participation levels fluctuate in response to aggregate changes in the political, economic, and social environment. We also posit that the direction of aggregate levels of black civic participation is predictable from macro-level forces in the economic, social, and political spheres that push and pull aggregate levels of black participation. These claims are explicitly tested in the rest of the book. We now turn to providing a more historically grounded explanation for our theory of countervailing forces and speculate how specific economic, social, and political factors affect the direction of black civic participation before and after the modern civil rights movement.

4

Echoes of Black Civic Activism

Historical Foundations and Longitudinal Considerations

> Time is not a river. Time is a pendulum . . . intricate patterns of recurrence in history.
>
> Arna Bontemps

The history of African-American political struggle has witnessed periods of progression and stagnation. As we documented in the previous chapter, our aggregate-level measures of black civic and political participation have demonstrated volatility during the post–civil rights era. Our analysis of social, economic, and political trends affecting black communities in the post–civil rights era also shows that black communities have experienced political progress as well as social and economic setbacks. Merging social, economic, and political trend data with aggregate-level measurements of black civic activity allows us to test empirically our theory of countervailing forces, which argues that social, economic, and political forces "push-and-pull" black civic participation.

In this chapter, we examine the historical foundations of the push and pull of black civic activism by considering how macro forces influenced black civic life from Reconstruction, the period in which African-American men were bought into the political system in the later part of the nineteenth century, to the dawn of the modern civil rights era, a period that set the stage for black political access and incorporation into mainstream political life in the late twentieth century. This historical analysis provides an illustrative backdrop to the ways in which macro forces have shaped black civic participation over time. As the historical evidence suggests, the push and pull of disfranchisement, industrialization, war, migration, economic depression, and partisan realignments have created both barriers and opportunities for black civic participation.

Because the majority of the black population was excluded from the American polity for most of the twentieth century, our consideration of macro political forces in the pre–civil rights period examines a different set of political factors than those that operate in the post–civil rights era. By the late nineteenth century, African Americans were both politically and economically marginalized in American life, having been stripped of political power and confined to a life of semiservitude as agricultural workers. For the first half of the twentieth century, African Americans – the majority of whom still lived in the South – were second-class citizens, serving as passive objects in the politics of white supremacy in the South rather than active citizens in the polity (Key 1949; Bunche 1973). In 1941, on the eve of the nation's entry into World War II, there were only thirty-three blacks in elective office; virtually all these officials were elected to office from black communities in the North (Jaynes and Williams 1989, 238). Consequently, African Americans were neither empowered nor incorporated into national politics.

Nonetheless, macro forces did make it possible for blacks to become important constituencies in urban political machines in northern cities and, by midcentury, blacks were critical constituencies in presidential politics in Northeastern and Midwestern states. What made these shifts in political influence possible were changes in macro social and economic forces such as the collapse of the cotton economy in the South, the mechanization of agricultural labor, labor shortages in the North during two world wars, and black migration to cities in states that were important to the outcome of presidential contests (McAdam 1982).

Though we do not have aggregate-level measures of black civic participation prior to the 1970s, the historical record suggests that a combination of macro forces in the economic, social, and political environments influenced the ebb and flow of black civic activity during the first half of the twentieth century. The tug-of-war between gradual political access and influence in the political system on the one side and social and economic fortunes on the other indicates that competition between the two forces for influence on black civic activity advantaged expanding social and economic opportunities in black communities. Despite the weakness and, in many cases, the absence of black political empowerment in black communities after Reconstruction and between the two world wars, the upward economic mobility of blacks, brought on by migration and the transformation of agricultural laborers into industrial workers, sustained and nurtured black civic life from the fall of Reconstruction to the rise of the modern civil rights movement.

Economic progress in the lives of African Americans contributed to the development and stability of the NAACP, Masonic organizations, the all-black Brotherhood of Sleeping Car Porters union, and activist church congregations in urban communities, clearing the way for the activism that emerged during the modern civil rights movement decades later. Thus, in contrast to our speculations about the opposing forces of politics and economics on black civic participation in the post–civil rights era, the historical evidence suggests that social and economic advancements in the lives of African Americans countered the negative effects of black political exclusion and marginality in the polity during most of the pre–civil rights period. By the start of the 1970s, these two opposing forces had reversed course. Greater political access and influence in the American polity in the aftermath of the civil rights movement pulled black participation upward, while negative economic and social forces in modern American life pushed black participation downward.

Although the set of countervailing forces differ in the pre– and post–civil rights eras, paying attention to how macro forces historically influenced black civic participation sheds light on the dynamics of black civic participation over time. In the pre–modern period, we examine factors such as black voter disfranchisement, urbanization, industrialization, and wars that provided barriers to and opportunities for black civic activism. In the modern period, we examine factors such as black office-holding, partisan control of the White House, black unemployment, inequality within the black population, inflation, and the economic consequences of job competition from immigrants. Again, understanding modern forces in the context of historical trends provides guidance in uncovering the push-and-pull dynamics of black civic participation in the post–civil rights era. Following a discussion of historical dynamics in black activism, the second section of this chapter considers the forces affecting aggregate-level changes in our measures of black civic participation from 1973 to 1994 by mapping the economic, social, and political "shocks" in our trend data to the aggregate-level fluctuations in black civic participation we estimate from the Roper surveys. The chapter concludes with a discussion of the benefits and limitations of using various methodological approaches to explain shifts in black civic participation over time.

HISTORICAL DYNAMICS IN THE STUDY OF RACE AND AMERICAN POLITICS

Research on race and political development has demonstrated how historical forces such as wars, partisan realignments, the construction of social policies, and the nation's economic fortunes have influenced the struggle for racial equality in the United States (Carmines and Stimson 1989; King 1995; Lieberman 1998; Klinkner and Smith 1999; Iton 2000; Kryder 2000; Williams 2003). In their sweeping history of racial reform in the United States, Phillip Klinkner and Rogers Smith argue that racial progress has occurred in short periods in American history when there have been large-scale wars requiring African-American participation, when those wars have forced the nation to live up to its inclusive, egalitarian values, and when wars occurred alongside domestic social movements that placed pressure on the state. Klinkner and Smith argue that racial reform in American history has exhibited a pattern of "two steps forward, (and) one step back," where steps toward reform have come in "concentrated bursts of ten to fifteen years," while setbacks in progress have covered "a period of sixty to seventy-five years" (Klinkner and Smith 1999, 5). They estimate that "the normal experience of the typical black person in U.S. history has been to live in a time of stagnation and decline of progress toward racial equality" (Klinkner and Smith 1999, 8).

Studies in race and American political development have offered historical perspectives on how racial exclusion influenced the direction of American political institutions and white political attitudes, but less research has focused on how macro dynamics have shaped the rise and decline of black civic and political participation over time. Doug McAdam's path-breaking work on the modern civil rights movement is an exception. In his study of the evolution of the modern civil rights movement, McAdam analyzed changes in the political environment, the strength and weakness of indigenous black institutions and organizations, and changes in the level of optimism and pessimism in black communities from Reconstruction to the end of the modern civil rights movement. The analysis is historical in its focus, but McAdam also statistically estimates the effects of macro social, economic, and political forces such as the gross national product (GNP), changes in the urbanization of the black population, the number of favorable Supreme Court decisions, declines in foreign immigration, the industrial demand for black labor, and black gains in education on the viability of black civic life. He shows that these macro-level forces either directly or indirectly influenced the growth of NAACP chapters in the first half of the twentieth century, a growth that would facilitate full-scale black activism by the late 1950s and early 1960s (McAdam 1982, 114).

In our analysis of the rise and decline of black civic and political participation, we do not see black activism following a linear pattern, where activism gradually rises in the aftermath of the civil war and reaches a plateau during the height of the civil rights movement in the 1960s. Rather we see – as evidenced by McAdam's work on the evolution of the modern civil rights movement – that black activism is influenced by the expansion and contraction of political opportunities and changes in the social and economic conditions that affect black communities in particular historical moments. Hence, our brief survey of black activism during Reconstruction/post-Reconstruction, the inter-War years, and the Second World War/post–Second World War years puts black civic participation at the center of our analysis and considers how macro forces shaped the contours of black civic activity during the last decades of the nineteenth century and for most of the twentieth century.

RECONSTRUCTION, POST-RECONSTRUCTION, AND BLACK CIVIC PARTICIPATION

The nation's first attempt at creating a true racial democracy in the United States fostered black civic and political participation during Reconstruction. To be sure, black freedmen in the North developed churches, Masonic organizations, and mutual aid societies prior to the

Civil War (Franklin 1980). However, Reconstruction allowed African Americans to create national civic, social, and religious organizations that would connect blacks across the nation. Indeed, the expansion and consolidation of black civic life during the Reconstruction years (1865–77) developed a civic infrastructure in black communities that would last for generations. This period witnessed substantial shifts in the political environment, where black men were, for the first time, included in the polity, only to be excluded from the public sphere by the end of the same century. In the aftermath of emancipation, African Americans were actively involved in political life, attending state constitutional conventions and participating in explicitly political organizations such as the Union Leagues, which supported Republican Party politics (Foner 1988).

Although black men attained the right to vote, the opportunities to participate in the polity were not restricted to men, nor were they confined to adults. As Elsa Barkley Brown observes in her analysis of African-American civic life in post–Civil War Richmond, Virginia, "in the immediate post-emancipation era black Richmonders enacted their understandings of democratic political discourse through mass meetings attended and participated in (including voting) by men, women and children and through mass participation in Republican Party conventions. They carried these notions of political participation into the state Capitol engaging from the gallery in the debates on the constitutional convention floor" (1994, 109).

What followed in the succeeding years of Reconstruction was the nation's first experience with an interracial democracy in which blacks temporarily gained political access but were not incorporated into the political system. Between 1865 and 1876, over 2,000 African-American men were elected to public office as members of Congress, state legislators, sheriffs, justices of the peace, and constables (Foner 1993). But black access and influence in the political system was short-lived. By way of judicial interpretations that undermined the intent of Reconstruction's constitutional amendments, compromises made by the Republican Party to become electorally competitive with Democrats for white votes, and through outright violence, the white "redeemers" in the South and the institutions of national governance converged into an all-out assault on the limited, though important, gains Reconstruction wrought for African Americans (Logan 1968;

Foner 1988; Frymer 1999). These political factors were reinforced by blacks' economic dependency on southern white landowners. By the end of the nineteenth century, political setbacks had led to what historian Rayford W. Logan dubbed as the "the nadir," or lowest point, in African Americans' quest for social and political rights since Emancipation.

Despite political setbacks and the economic marginality of the freedmen, blacks built schools, developed mutual aid societies, consolidated national religious denominations, and created racial uplift organizations such as the National Association of Colored Women's Clubs (Franklin 1980). At the same time that blacks were being removed from the nation's official public sphere, black civic life outside the boundaries of electoral politics flourished. For instance, Theda Skocpol and Jennifer Lynn Oser's analysis of the rise and fall of black membership in Masonic orders such as the Prince Hall Masons, the Odd Fellows, the Elks, and the Order of the Eastern Stars (women's auxiliary) shows substantial growth during the late nineteenth century. As the authors illustrate, black fraternalism in the South and the North exploded between the 1880s and 1900, exceeding the participation of northern whites and southern whites by 1895. Despite the dim prospects for participation in the polity, the black Masonic orders cultivated civic skills of both black men and women that would eventually spill over into electoral politics when opportunities for participation expanded (Harris 1999a). Skocpol and Oser observe:

> The opportunities fraternal orders offered to African Americans for leadership and cooperation were unquestionably highly valued. On the civic and political side, participation in fraternal groups allowed otherwise suppressed African Americans to organize and assemble in public – in the North for parades and public celebrations of "Emancipation Day" and other special holidays . . . and in the South for funeral processions even in places where other public assemblages of African Americans were prohibited. (2005, 420)

Thus, Reconstruction and the post-Reconstruction period left an imprint on black civic participation. Without the building of religious and social institutions, which were crucial in providing civic skills to blacks' entry into politics during their migration North and during episodes of black protest in both regions during the inter-War years, the gradual movement toward direct political action in black communities would have occurred at a slower pace. As Eric Foner notes of the

Reconstruction and post-Reconstruction eras and their implications for social change in black communities, "the tide of change rose and then receded, but it left behind an altered landscape. The freedman's political and civil equality proved transitory, but the autonomous black family and a network of religious and social institutions survived the end of Reconstruction" (1988, 602). The survival of black civic life from the political disappointments of the post-Reconstruction era sowed the seeds of social change that accelerated black progress in the twentieth century.

BLACK CIVIC LIFE IN THE INTERWAR YEARS

Bracketed by the First World War, which encouraged the first large wave of black migration from the rural South to urban centers in the North and West, and World War II, which encouraged even larger waves of black migration, the inter-War period also witnessed the Great Depression, which reaped economic havoc throughout the nation and on African Americans who were already economically vulnerable. The macro force that had the greatest long-term effect on black civic life was the "Great Migration." As a report of black churches and voluntary associations in Chicago reported at the time of black migration North, low wages, destruction of cotton crops by the boll weevil, poor standards of living, and the lack of school facilities "pushed" blacks from the south while immigration restrictions during World War I, higher wages in the North, relatively better living conditions, and the opportunity to attend school "pulled" blacks out of the south (Drake 1940, 142).

Even though the post-Reconstruction era represented dim prospects for political organizing in black communities, blacks' northern migration led to expanded opportunities for African Americans to participate in electoral politics. An estimated 1.5 million African Americans left the South between 1900 and 1930, more than doubling the black population of urban enclaves such as Chicago, Detroit, Cleveland, New York, and Philadelphia (Higginbotham 1997, 134). The Great Migration set in motion civic engagement on several dimensions, including the first stages of black incorporation into urban political machines as well as participation in other forms of civic life such as labor union activities, membership in the local NAACP chapters, participation in protest campaigns against discrimination in housing and employment, and, most notably, participation in perhaps the largest black social movement in the twentieth century, Marcus Garvey's Universal Negro Improvement Association, which called for blacks to repatriate to Africa (Gosnell 1967; Meier and Rudwick 1989).

The expanding opportunities to participate in electoral activities were initiated by political parties, which competed for black voters in cities such as Cleveland, New York, Chicago, and St. Louis (Gosnell 1967; Bunche 1973). Black participation in electoral politics went beyond registering preferences at the voting booth. As Harold Gosnell's study of black politics during the 1920s and 1930s shows, African Americans served as precinct captains, ran for political office, and attended political rallies. His description of one political meeting on the city's South Side during the inter-War period reveals the level of political interest in Chicago's black communities:

> A Negro audience is attentive, enthusiastic, patient, good natured and content to sit many hours on uncomfortable seats. When a speaker says something which strikes a popular chord, they shout, clap, or wave programs, hats, or hands in the air. Politics is evidently something which is very close to their daily life and their racial aspirations. They feel that their jobs, their freedom, their right to vote, their happiness, their very lives almost are at stake unless their candidates win. (1967, 147)

The inter-War years also shifted the partisan alliances of African Americans from the Republican to the Democratic Party (Drake and Cayton [1945] 1993; Weiss 1983). The social welfare policies of the New Deal wooed black voters away from the Republican Party, bringing northern blacks into national politics. With the migration of blacks into key electoral states in the Northeast (New York and Pennsylvania), Midwest (Illinois, Michigan, Ohio), and West (California), northern African Americans were given incentives to participate in local, state, and national politics. Black voters became such a critical component of the Democratic Party's New Deal coalition that, by the 1940 presidential election, the party had included an antidiscrimination plank in its platform for the first time in the party's history. The plank proclaimed that the party would "uphold due process and equal protection of the laws of every citizen, regardless of race, creed or color" (Moon 1948, 31).

Migration encouraged participation in protest activities. In their study of Chicago, St. Clair Drake and Horace A. Cayton record how the organization of discontent in Chicago's black belt took on a variety of strategies during the 1920s and 1930s. These tactics included picketing and boycotting department stores and trade unions that refused to hire blacks, filing lawsuits against realtors who practiced discrimination through racially restrictive covenants, organizing rent strikes against high rents, and initiating consumer boycotts against companies that refuse to hire blacks (Drake and Cayton [1945] 1993).

The urbanization of the black population created opportunities for organized protest in the North and South during the inter-War years. Protests such as the "Don't-Buy-Where-You-Can't-Work" campaigns, which boycotted and picketed department stores that discriminated against black workers during the Depression, took place in northern communities such as Toledo, Cleveland, Detroit, Philadelphia, Boston, and St. Louis and in southern cities such as Norfolk, Richmond, Atlanta, and New Orleans (Meier and Rudwick 1989). Migration and urbanization in the South also contributed to the growth of NAACP chapters and to the emergence of greater numbers of socially active black churches. As Doug McAdam notes, "larger concentrations of blacks in urban areas who possessed the characteristics associated with membership and were afforded a measure of protection from the more virulent forms of racism that probably inhibited organizing in rural areas" facilitated the strengthening of black civic and religious life in southern cities during the period (1982, 105).

Despite the political advances African Americans made during the inter-War years, economic forces such as the Depression weakened aspects of black civic life. For instance, Theda Skocpol and Jennifer Oser document the erosion and extinction of black Masonic membership during the Depression, noting that black lodges were more fragile than white ones because black members were more likely to face "greater economic privations, which meant that in times of economic stress it was harder for black lodges to keep up collections of membership dues" (2004, 411). Nonetheless, migration, relatively greater economic security in the North, and the opening of political access for northern blacks facilitated the growth and stability of black civic life during the inter-War years.

WORLD WAR II, THE COLD WAR, AND BLACK CIVIC LIFE

The Second World War accelerated the social and economic progress that African Americans gradually made during the inter-War years. National mobilization during the Second World War and the ideological contradictions of the Cold War provided moral and tactical leverage for the African-American freedom struggle (Klinkner and Smith 1999; Kryder 2000; Dudziak 2002). On the economic side, the war expanded employment opportunities for African Americans in the industrial sector, as the wartime economy needed black workers. These economic opportunities not only provided material resources for blacks to enhance and sustain their civic participation, the war also provided an opportunity for African Americans to mobilize politically in opposition to racial discrimination in government employment.

As part of the protest strategy that would characterize the civil rights movement during the 1950s and 1960s, labor leader A. Phillip Randolph threatened a march on Washington during the early years of the war that called on 10,000 African Americans to protest employment discrimination in the war industries. Randolph used the threat of a march to send a message to President Roosevelt that "loyal Negro-American citizens demand to work and fight for our country" (Jaynes and Williams 1989, 63). Because of the March on Washington Movement, Roosevelt signed an executive order forbidding racial discrimination in war industry jobs. Executive order 8802 was one of the most significant presidential actions directed toward African Americans after Reconstruction. Other positive signals from government on the federal level encouraged black activism. The Supreme Court began to give favorable civil rights rulings, including decisions that outlawed the all-white Democratic Party primaries in the South, racially restrictive housing covenants, and separate-but-unequal discrimination in higher education during the 1940s and 1950s. These rulings culminated with the 1954 *Brown Decision*, which declared that separate schools for blacks and whites were unconstitutional. Favorable government actions expanded a sense of optimism in black communities during the post–World War II years, which indirectly contributed to protest action (McAdam 1982).

In addition to favorable government action, African Americans continued to be a swing constituency in presidential elections during the postwar years, especially during the fiercely contested 1948 presidential election. That year the Democrats called for racial reforms with a far more aggressive antidiscrimination plank than the 1940 party platform. The 1948 platform called for the party's opposition to the poll tax, a commitment to anti-lynching legislation, and support for the Fair Employment Practices Commission which was created to monitor employment discrimination during the Roosevelt administration. The antidiscrimination platform prompted the Dixiecrat candidacy of Strom Thurman and began the gradual exodus of white southerners from the Democratic Party.

Progress was also made with black representation in Congress. The immediate post–World War II years saw the growth of the largest contingent of blacks in Congress since Reconstruction, with the reelections of William Dawson of Chicago and the election of Adam Clayton Powell of Harlem and Charles Diggs of Detroit during the 1940s and 1950s. By the beginning of the 1970s, the numbers of blacks in the House of Representatives had tripled, ushering in the possibility of black incorporation.

In addition to advances in national politics, favorable court decisions, and the ideological contradictions of the Cold War that highlighted the mistreatment of African Americans (as the federal government promoted democracy internationally), black migration and urbanization would continue to strengthen black civil society. As Doug McAdam documents, black migration to southern cities during the Second World War contributed to the explosive growth of NAACP chapters in the region. After the Depression, over 70 percent of new NAACP chapters were located in the South and approximately 85 percent of those chapters were situated in urban areas (1982, 104–5). Additionally, the transformation of black church life in the post–World War II era also enhanced the civic capacity of black communities in the urban south. As McAdam reports, 70 percent of black congregants in the South during the 1930s attended "small, weak, and rural" churches; by the mid-1950s more than half of black congregants were members of larger black congregations, a trend that began in the North during the first large wave of black migration during the First World War (1982, 100). These larger congregations, many of which had full-time ministers, nurtured the civic skills of African Americans that were mobilized for protest during the civil rights movement (Harris 1999a).

The post–World War II period also saw growth in black college attendance. Enrollment in black colleges doubled between 1940 and 1950, with nearly 75,000 African Americans attending college by midcentury (McAdam 1982, 102). Given the number of black World War II veterans who pursued higher education through the GI Bill at majority white institutions, the number of blacks enrolled in college more than likely exceeded 75,000. During the 1940s and 1950s, black and white college students in the Congress for Racial Equality (CORE) held demonstrations protesting segregated practices at lunch counters, restaurants, department stores, and movie theaters in northern cities. By the early 1960s, college students at historically black colleges were the vanguard of the sit-in movements throughout the South (McAdam 1982). Economic, social, and political forces that developed during the Second World War and decades after had a profound effect on the development of the modern civil rights movement.

As our brief historical survey suggests, macro processes in the economic, social, and political environment contribute to the historical development of African-American civic activism. Changes in the social, economic, and political fortunes of black communities have influenced the rise and decline of black civic engagement from Reconstruction to the modern civil rights movement. These forces include economic and social forces such as migration, industrialization, urbanization, "hot and cold wars," and the expansion and contraction of political opportunities that ease or restrict black participation in the American political system. We now examine how changes in the political, social, and economic environment influence black civic participation in the post–civil rights era. Even though the macro forces in the modern period are different, they nonetheless have similar effects on the dynamics of black civic life in the modern era.

MACRO FORCES IN THE POST–CIVIL RIGHTS ERA

We consider the countervailing forces of empowerment and social and economic distress on aggregate-level changes in black civic participation by speculating on how these forces push and pull black civic participation over time. As in the case of macro forces prior to the civil rights movement, such as migration, urbanization, and industrialization, we see macro forces contributing to fluctuations in black civic participation in the post–civil rights era. As we demonstrated in Chapter 3 in our discussion of patterns in black civic participation from 1973 to 1994, aggregate levels of black civic participation have been stable over the period. But, despite stable patterns in black participation in the post–civil rights era, there have been fluctuations that might be accounted for by responses in the social, economic, and political environment.

Figure 4.1 shows changes in our composite measure of black civic participation in the twenty-one-year period accompanied by political empowerment and social and economic distress indicators. Our theory maintains that empowerment and distress have opposing effects on black civic participation, either pulling black participation upward, in the case of empowerment, or pushing black participation downward, in the case of distress. Indicators of empowerment are represented at the top of the figure, while indicators of distress are at the bottom. At the beginning of the time period, we see two indicators from our two sets of forces that possibly work against each other. In early 1973, there were approximately 2,600 black elected officials in the country during a period when the aggregate mean of black participation was a little more than 0.8 political acts. During this same period, black unemployment was at 9.4 percent, the lowest rate between 1973 and 1994. In this case, empowerment and distress are relatively favorable for black participation, with increasing empowerment, pulling participation substantially upward, and relatively less distress pushing black participation slightly downward.

Based on our theory and expectations, the Carter presidency should have pushed black civic participation forward because of positive signals that a Democratic presidency would send to African Americans about the relative likelihood of having their policy preferences acted upon. However, we see a lull in aggregate levels of black civic participation during the Carter years. During these same years, the nation experiences historic highs in price inflation (see Figure 2.5), in which sharp rises in the cost of goods and services may have eroded any benefits from a Democratic presidency, moving black participation upward. In the mid-1980s, we also see two forces possibly working at odds in affecting aggregate-level changes in black civic participation. There is a surge in black civic participation in 1984 during the presidential candidacy of Jesse Jackson. As a force of empowerment, Jackson's

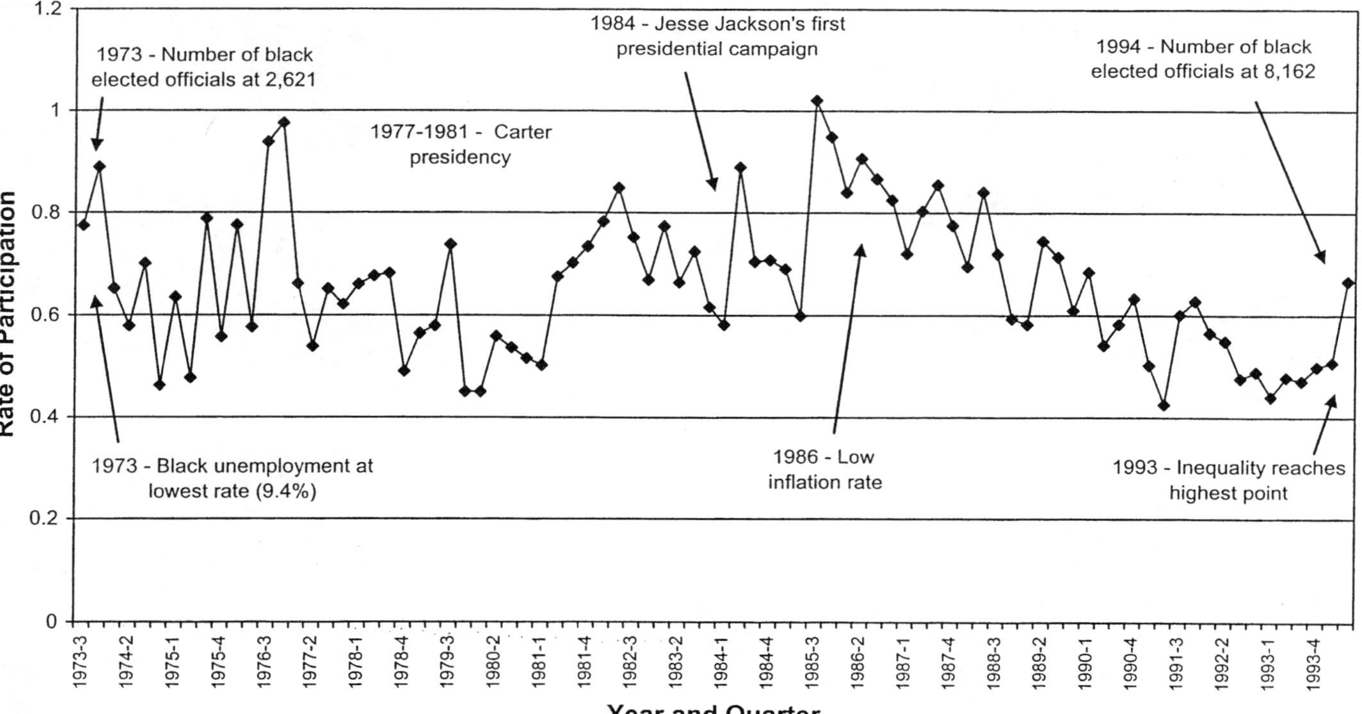

FIGURE 4.1. Civic participation index, 1973–1994. Source: Roper Social and Political Trends Data.

1984 candidacy should pull aggregate-levels of black civic participation upward, which suggests that his presidency overpowered negative social and economic forces in black communities that pushed participation downward, such as unemployment and labor force competition from immigrants. However, we also see a sharp rise in black civic participation around 1986, where aggregate black participation reaches a high of slightly more than one political act. This occurs at approximately the same period when inflation is at its lowest point during the twenty-one-year period. As a distress factor, inflation during this period could have had less of a deteriorating effect on aggregate-level black participation given historic lows in prices and services.

Toward the end of our timeline, we see two more forces possibly working against each other. As a force of empowerment, the number of black elected officials tops 8,000, quadrupling the number of black elected officials that existed at the beginning of our survey period. We see a dive in aggregate-level changes of black civic participation as the number of black elected officials continues to inch upward. At the same time, we also see that a distress factor, income dispersion among African Americans, reached its highest point in the twenty-one-year period. From the perspective of our theory of countervailing forces, black office-holding and greater income dispersion within the black community are opposing forces pushing and pulling black civic participation. As the stories of the fictional families of the Jeffersons and the Evans suggest, the widening class differences among blacks, which peaked in the early 1990s, might be working against black civic participation despite the greater numbers of black elected officials.

As we discussed in our exploration of the push-and-pull factors on black participation prior to the civil rights movement, macro forces in the economic, social, and political spheres operate as opportunities for and barriers to black participation. Our longitudinal data allows us to test simultaneously the opportunities created by empowerment and the barriers resulting from social and economic distress. Rather than test these countervailing forces in one year, using individual reports to make inferences about the participation of blacks as a group, we estimate the tug-of-war between empowerment and distress from the early years of black incorporation into mainstream politics during the 1970s to the early 1990s, when the Democratic Party elects Ron Brown the first African American to lead the party. In the next chapter, we provide estimates of empowerment and distress factors on various modes of black civic participation. But before we move to our multivariate analysis, we briefly discuss our methodological strategy for considering time in our study.

A NOTE ON ESTIMATING TIME

Our historical and empirical results might lead to the expectation that we would use a conventional time series technique to understand how various political, economic, and social distress factors push and pull black civic participation up or down in the post–civil rights era.[1] In our present study, this research strategy would be beneficial because it would allow us to isolate the specific effects of distress and empowerment shocks at particular moments in time in our civic participation series. In short, time series analysis takes into account the fact that social and political phenomena may change over time, increasing or decreasing depending on changes in the environment. Political scientists typically use time series analysis to study how citizens' partisanship preferences change over time, to illustrate how liberal or conservative attitudes in the electorate vary across decades, or to study changing patterns of expenditures on domestic social welfare programs.

There are a number of issues to be aware of when considering the use of time series analysis as a methodological approach (Gujarati 1995; Enders 2004). To begin with, researchers must have a good theoretical argument establishing that time matters. In other words, it should be clear that a relationship exists between what is being analyzed and the factors being used to explain changes in them. In the case of political behavior studies, analysts would also want relatively even sample sizes across the period under examination. Moreover, there should be a clear indication of the direction of causality over time, that is, *a* causes *b* over time. There should also be some evidence that occurrences over time are correlated (i.e., what occurs at time period *a* is related to what occurs at time period *b*). Finally, there should be a sense of how much the explanatory factors impact the movement trends in what is being explained over time. Unfortunately, in our analysis of black civic activism over time, our data does not meet all of these criteria.

[1] We present the results from three time series models in Appendix C.

We certainly have strong theoretical arguments for explaining black civic activism over time, and our data covers multiple points over time, satisfying two of the criteria we outlined. However, our data do not adequately meet the remaining criteria necessary to conduct a true time series analysis.

Our first concern is the structure of the Roper Trend data. The sample sizes vary across our eighty-four quarters. In thinking about how black civic participation fluctuates over time, we are mindful of the fact that the number of black respondents that we use to estimate aggregate levels of black participation varies slightly. For example, one-third of the quarters we examine have fewer than 438 black respondents. Another third of our quarters contain between 443 and 622 respondents. The final third of our quarters contains between 623 and 835 black respondents. These variations in the sample sizes of black respondents must be taken into account as we try to explain movements in black participation over time.

We also have a concern about making comparisons about the relative effects of our empowerment and distress measures. Recall that we are interested in understanding black civic participation from the viewpoint of a tug-of-war between black empowerment and social and economic distress forces. Simply put, we want to make a number of straightforward comparisons about which variables matter more for determining aggregate level changes in black civic participation at particular moments in time. Taken together, these two concerns point us in a slightly different methodological direction. To account for these limitations, we instead use generalized least squares regression analysis to investigate changes in black civic activism. We address the strengths of our methodological decision next.

GLS regression is more appropriate than a traditional time series technique for addressing our theoretical questions regarding the relative effects of black empowerment and social distress on African-American civic behavior. GLS analysis allows us to see which of our independent variables have a greater effect on black civic participation. For instance, in discussing our findings, we would like to know if the Jackson campaigns in 1984 and 1988, increases in black office-holding, or gains in black college enrollments pull black civic participation upward. On the other hand, we would like to know if social and economic distress factors, such as increasing inequality within black communities and rising levels of inflation and black unemployment, pull black participation downward. By explicitly examining the effects of the tug-of-war of structural factors on black civic participation, we can determine which sets of factors are more important for explaining black civic engagement in the post–civil rights era.

The greatest advantage of GLS regression is that it allows us to consider variations in the number of black respondents and estimate the effects of our explanatory variables. Our use of GLS models is also supported by our examination of how the Roper data are structured as we move from 1973 to 1994. All of these tests suggest that GLS models are appropriate for studying changes in black civic participation over time.[2] Additionally, our study represents an improvement over previous cross-sectional studies that employ the 1984 and 1996 National Black Election Study, the 1993 National Black Politics Study, or the 1982 and 1987 General Social Surveys to understand black participation. These surveys and the analyses that have been produced from them only provide an episodic portrait of black civic and political life. In contrast, our study permits us to "connect the dots" in a unique way from 1973 to 1994 and allows us to explore how aggregate levels of black civic participation changed over time while black communities were being affected by economic, social, and political change. In the next chapter, we provide some answers.

[2] We performed two tests on our black civic participation model, the Durbin–Watson test and a plot of the residuals over time. The results of the Durbin-Watson test were inconclusive, indicating that we cannot determine if strong autocorrelation is present in our model. In addition, our residual plots indicate that there exists the probability that only slight autocorrelation is present in our participation models.

5

Shifting Forces

Modeling Changes in Post–Civil Rights Black Activism

> If we are serious, the black politics of Gary must accept major responsibility for creating both the atmosphere and program for fundamental, far ranging change in America.
>
> Activist, National Black Political Convention, 1972

> The new civil rights movement must reframe its strategy around combating civil death, pushing for meaningful, winnable reforms that increase the civic capacities of oppressed people, permitting them to assume greater roles in determining society's future.
>
> Manning Marable, *The Great Wells of Democracy*, 2002

In the previous chapter, we argued that the macro-level forces of empowerment and distress act as counterweights to each other, pulling black activism upward or pushing it downward as social, economic, and political opportunities were created by some factors and constrained by others. We also presented the historical and methodological rationale for the modeling choices we make in our analysis of post–civil rights black activism. In this chapter, we use statistical models to examine how well these sets of factors explain changes in aggregate levels of black activism from 1973 and 1994. The first part of the chapter describes trends in civic activism for blacks as a group, by region, and by gender. We then present the results of our GLS models of composite participation, political work, and organizational work, which show consistent evidence of a tug-of-war between black political empowerment on the one hand and social and economic distress on the other. We find that the negative push of social and economic distress on black activism all but nullifies the positive pull of black political empowerment in the post–civil rights era. Later in the chapter, we turn our attention to the analysis of black activism by social class where we find that empowerment and distress factors operate differently for lower-status, working-class, and middle-class blacks.

DEMOGRAPHIC TRENDS IN BLACK CIVIC ACTIVISM

We now consider trends in black civic participation in the black population and across region and gender categories. As we noted in previous chapters, our measure of *Composite Participation* is an additive index that combines both political work and organizational work into one general measure of black activism. Our *Political Work Index* is an additive index of the following activities: attending a rally or speech, being a member of a political party, being a member of a political organization, and signing a petition. The *Organizational Work Index* is an additive index of the following: serving as an officer for an organization, serving on a committee for a local organization, making a speech, and attending a public meeting on town or school affairs.

As a starting point, we briefly discuss differences in black and white civic activism. Scholars of political participation have demonstrated that most Americans infrequently engage in civic activities (Putnam 2000; Burns, Schlozman, and Verba 2001, 70–1). Participation in political activities declined for both blacks and whites between 1973 and 1994, and blacks were considerably less likely to engage in political participation than whites (Rosenstone and Hansen 1993). Figure 5.1 reports the average rate of civic participation for blacks, whites, and the general population from 1973 to 1994. Even though the average American participated in one and a half political acts in 1973, that average had declined to slightly less than one act by 1994. Moreover, there are clear differences in the patterns of participation between blacks and whites. Blacks are considerably less likely to engage in civic activity than whites for all years. Indeed, the Roper data show that the average measure of black participation never exceeds one act for any of the years.

While the general population shows a gradual decline in aggregate levels of political participation, there is considerable volatility in rates

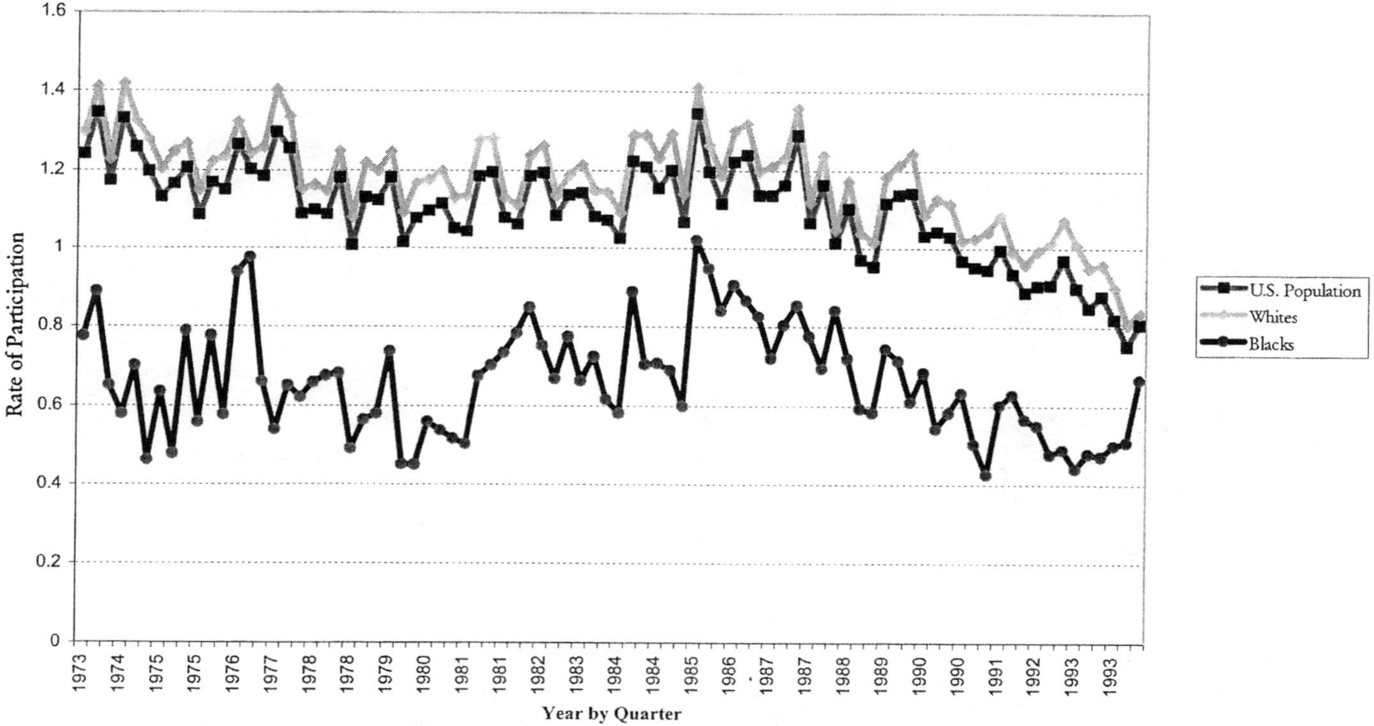

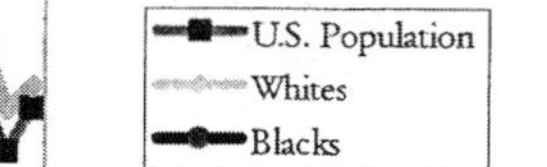

FIGURE 5.1. Composite participation index by race, 1973–1994.

of black participation when compared to whites and the general population. Declines and surges in the participation rate of blacks characterize the pattern between 1973 and 1988. We see a pattern of decline between the mid-1970s and the early 1980s; a surge, decline, and resurgence between 1983 and 1987; and a continuous decline after 1987. By the late 1980s, the decline in black participation matches the pattern of whites and the general population.

Figures 5.2–5.4 show quarterly changes in black composite participation, political work, and organizational work by region. As we see in Figure 5.2, trends in the composite participation index by region reveal a pattern of diminishing differences. Non-southern black composite participation peaked at 1.2 acts in the mid-1970s, while the peak for southern blacks in the late 1970s was not quite one act. Southern blacks experienced a second peak in composite participation in the early 1990s. The sharp decline in composite participation experienced by non-southern blacks in the late 1980s was mirrored by a less steep decline in participation by southern blacks, so that by the early 1990s, aggregate levels of composite participation were quite similar for both groups with southern blacks participating at slightly higher levels than non-southerners.

Figure 5.3 shows that regional differences in political work are apparent through the late 1980s, when declining black participation outside the South diminishes regional distinctions. Political work among southern blacks averaged between 0.1 and 0.3 political acts for most of the twenty-one-year period. Black southerners' participation in political work peaked again in 1986 and never returned to the lows experienced prior to 1984. Reaching a high point above 0.6 political acts in the mid-1970s, early 1980s, and mid-1980s, aggregate levels of political work among blacks outside the South surpassed southern blacks during most of the post–civil rights era. By the mid-1980s, non-southern black political work began a punctuated decline in 1986, falling below black southerners' political work in the early 1990s and dropping to a low of less than 0.2 acts a few years later.

Figure 5.4 shows that regional trends in black organizational work are less distinct by comparison than trends in political work and composite participation. For most of the three-decade period under examination, black organizational work ranged between 0.2 and 0.4 acts for both southerners and non-southerners. Organizational work by

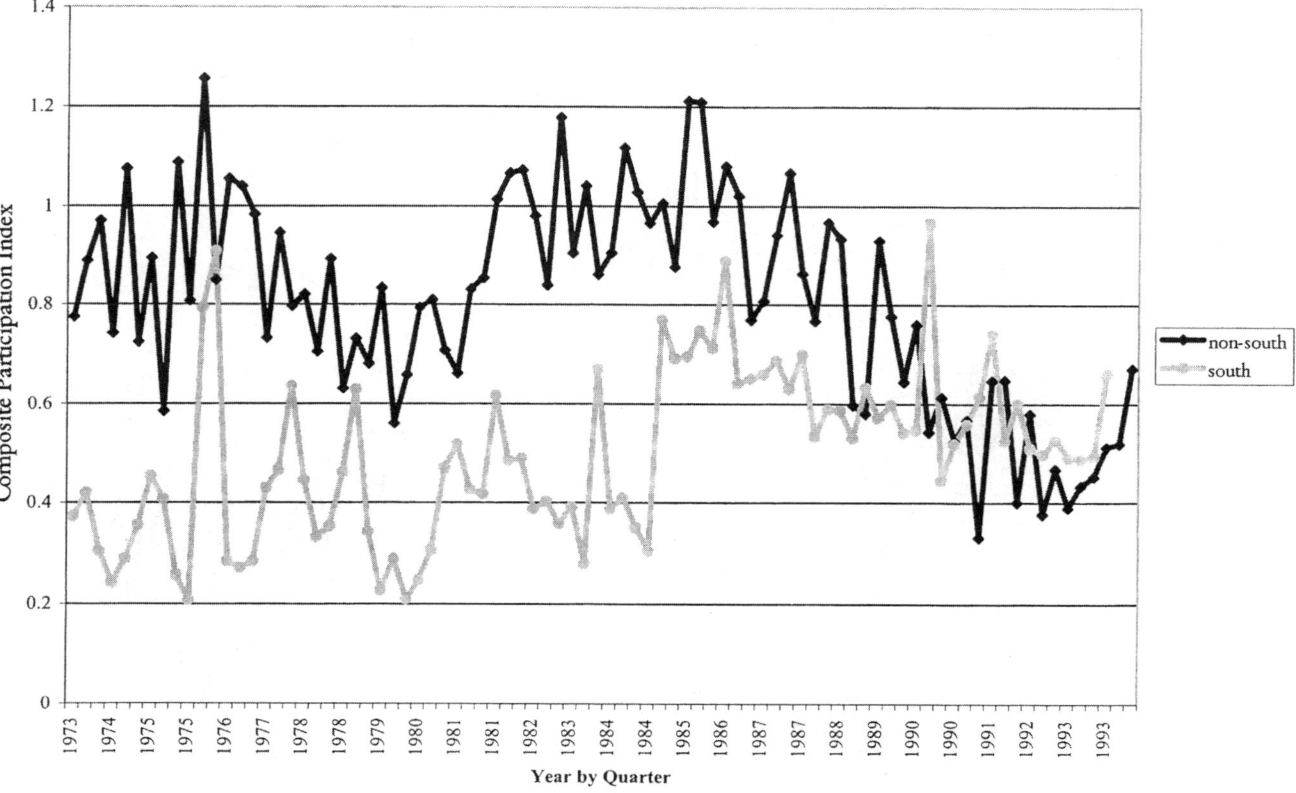

FIGURE 5.2. Composite participation index by region, 1973–1994.

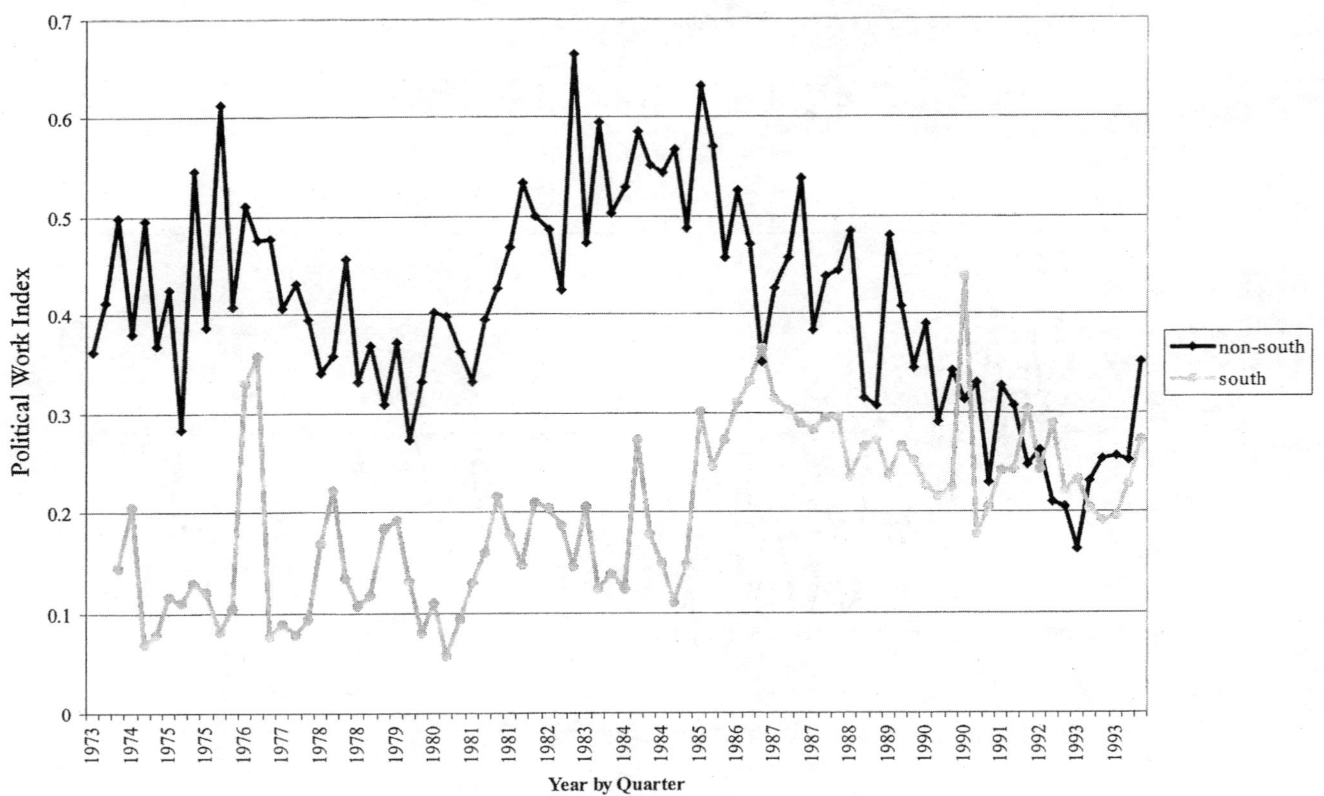

FIGURE 5.3. Political work by region, 1973–1994.

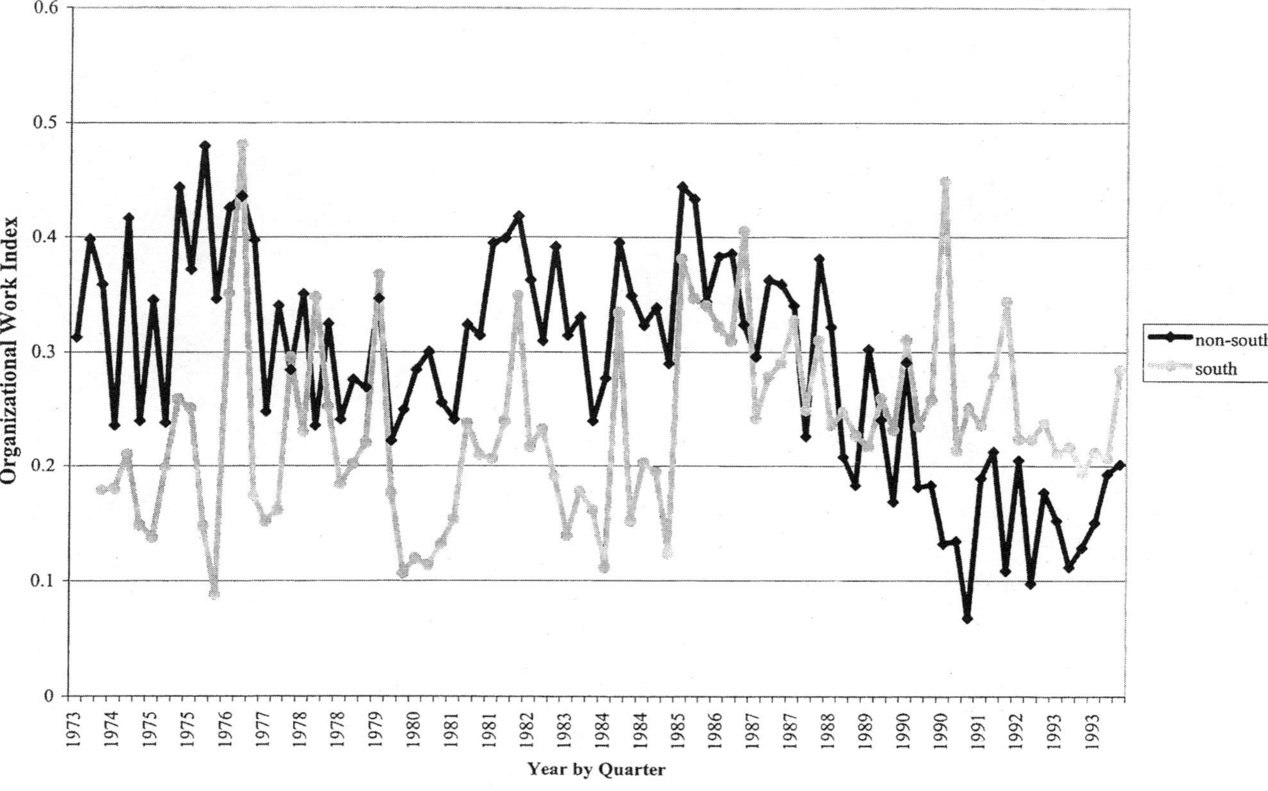

FIGURE 5.4. Organizational work by region, 1973–1994.

non-southerners slightly outpaced that of non-southerners until the mid-1980s when organizational work by non-southerners began a slow decline. Organizational work patterns for black southerners began to increase at about the same time, never again reaching the previous lows, and finally consistently outpaced non-southern organizational work in the early 1990s. These patterns demonstrate that despite evidence of the decreasing uniqueness of southern politics when compared to politics outside the region, we find distinct patterns of black civic participation in the south during the post–civil rights era.

We consider gender differences for several reasons. Black women are more likely to report voting in elections than black men, a pattern that might be replicated in nonvoting civic activity (Giddings 1984; Williams 1987). Moreover, black women are often grassroots organizers of political, community, and religious organizations though they may be less directly engaged in campaign activities (Giddings 1984; Robnett 1997; Harris 1999a, 154–75). Thus, empowerment and distress factors may affect the civic activism of black women and men differently. Figures 5.5 through 5.7 show changes in aggregate levels of composite participation, political work, and organizational work, respectively, by gender between 1973 and 1994.

Figure 5.5 shows that, with the exception of 1973, when black men's composite participation exceeded one participation act, gender differences in participatory activity have been small. Between 1973 and 1983, black men participated with only slightly more frequency than black women on average. Participation for both black men and women began a slow decline in the mid-1980s, demonstrating only minor shifts in participation rates in the later years of this study.

Figure 5.6 once again shows only minor variations in civic activity across gender. Averages in the political work of black men slightly exceeded that of black women between 1973 and 1983, but after the early 1980s, participation in political work varied little, with gradual declines in participation for both groups. Figure 5.6 shows a similar trend for organizational work, except that black women were more engaged in organizational work than black men between the mid-1970s and mid-1980s. After the mid-1980s, there were only slight differences in the organizational participation of men and women, although women had a slight edge over men.

Before we discuss the results of our statistical analysis, we will review our expectations about the effects of black political empowerment and

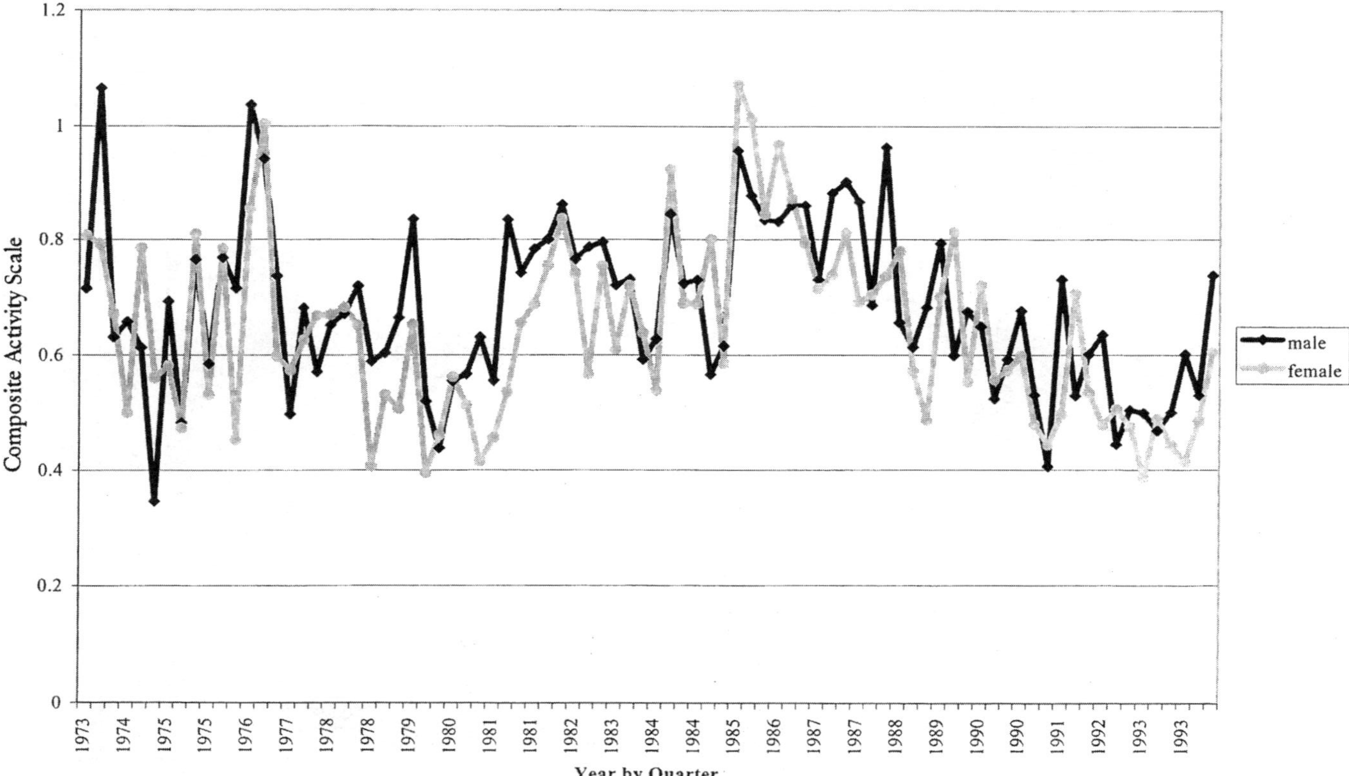

FIGURE 5.5. Composite participation index by gender, 1973–1994.

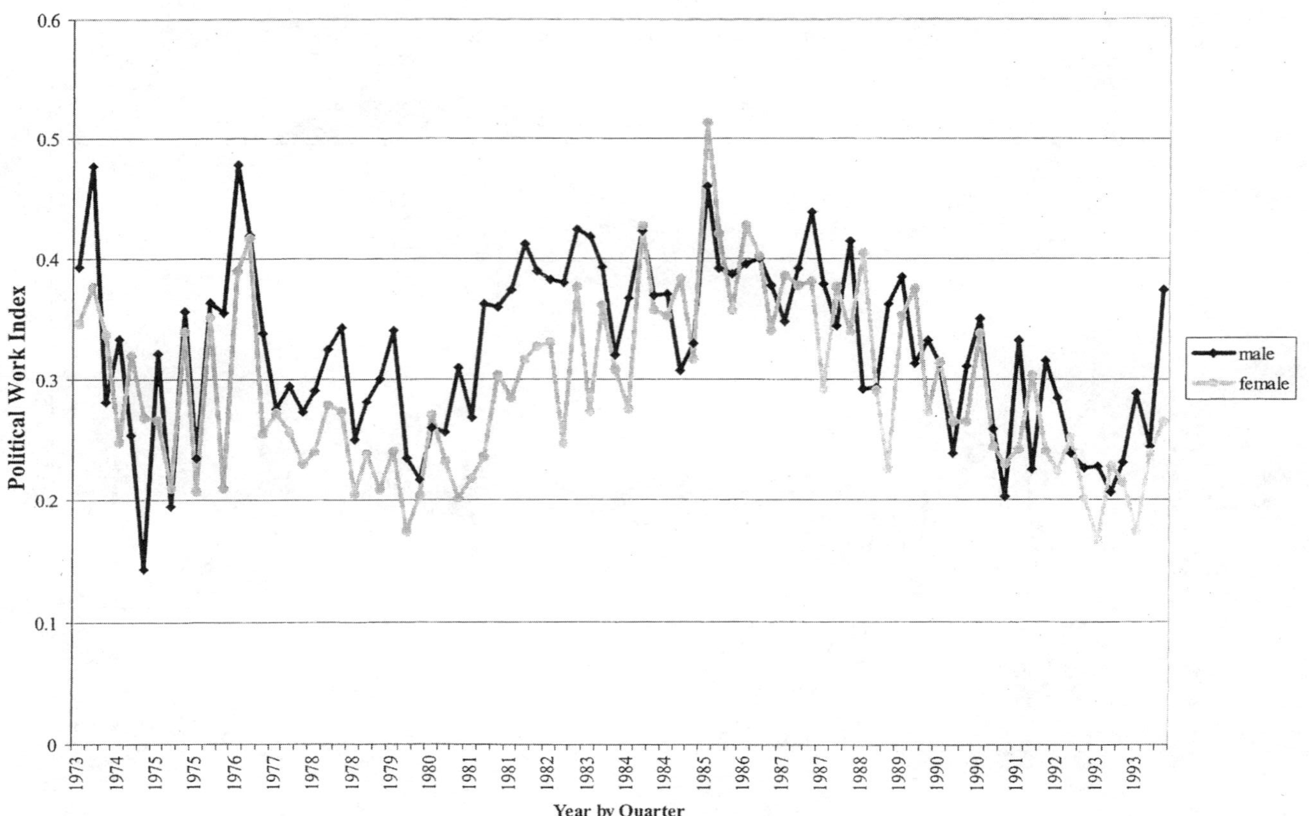

FIGURE 5.6. Political work by gender, 1973–1994.

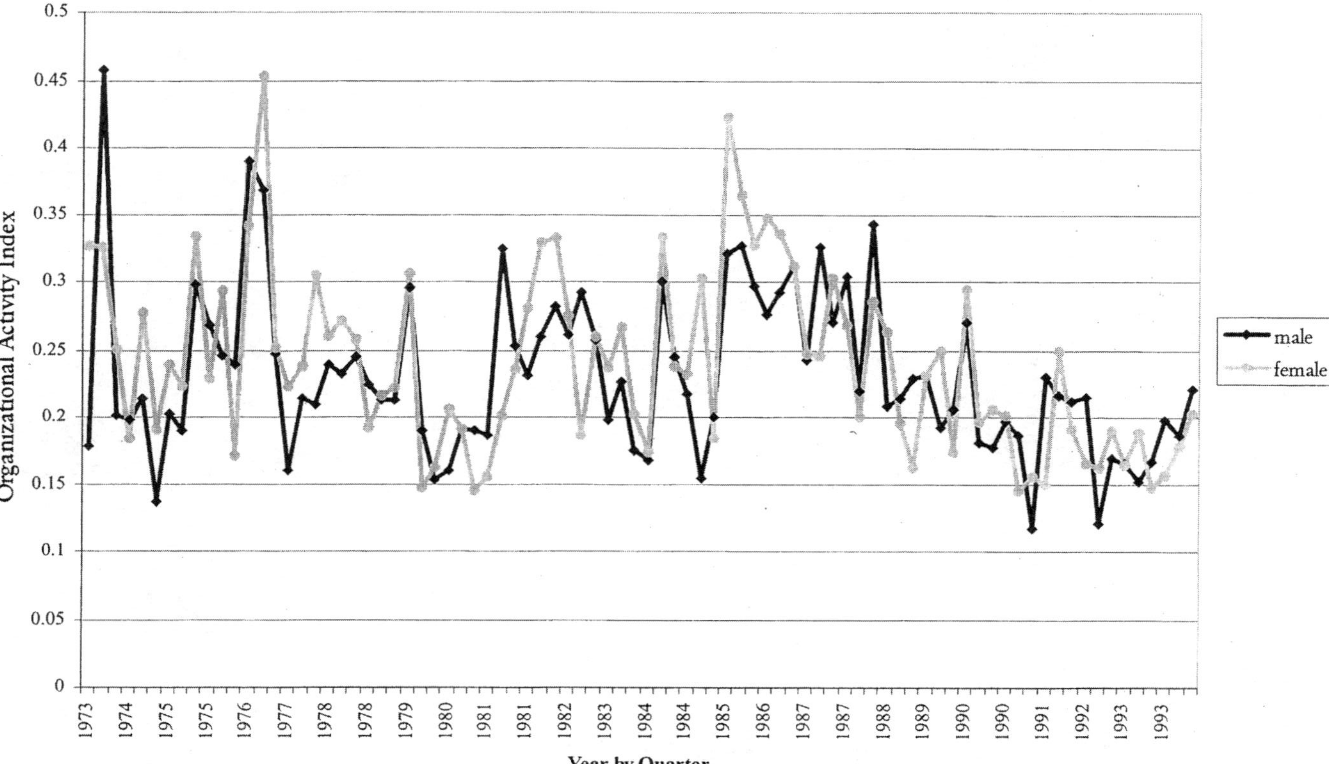

FIGURE 5.7. Organizational work by gender, 1973–1994.

social and economic distress on aggregate-level black participation.[1] Political empowerment, economic distress, and social distress may have different effects on our measures of activity because of regional or gender differences. Regional differences among blacks in voting may have implications for more demanding activities such as attending rallies, serving on committees in local organizations, or on participation activity more generally. Similarly, the same pattern of gender differences evidenced in black voting behavior (Alex-Assensoh and Stanford 1997) may translate into different explanations of nonvoting civic activism for black men and women.

MEASURES OF BLACK POLITICAL EMPOWERMENT

Throughout the book we have discussed the many ways that political empowerment may stimulate black civic activism. Recall that we consider four factors that measure the political empowerment of blacks in the post–civil rights era: a direct measure, the number of black elected officials for each year between 1973 and 1994, and three indirect measures, specifically the 1984 and 1988 Jesse Jackson presidential campaigns as a proxy measure for the impact of a viable black candidacy at the national level, whether a Democratic or Republican president controls the White House, and the year-to-year rate of black college enrollment.[2]

BLACK ELECTED OFFICIALS AT ALL LEVELS OF GOVERNMENT

We argue that increases in the number of black elected officials from the early 1970s to the early 1990s should positively affect black activism,

[1] Unfortunately, quarterly data for many of our explanatory variables do not exist (e.g., numbers of black elected officials, black college enrollments, and black income inequality). In order to maintain consistency across independent variables, we use yearly data rather than a mix of yearly and quarterly data. As a consequence, we use relatively (but not entirely) static measures to explain more variable quarterly behavior. Thus, our model may underestimate the impact of political empowerment and economic and social isolation on black nonvoting participation.

[2] Because the Roper survey asks respondents to report on their participation in the past year, the data are coded to match each quarter of aggregate civic activity to political, social, and economic indicators from the previous year to predict the quarterly variations in the dependent variable (e.g., quarterly responses from 1977 are predicted by macro-level measures from 1976).

pulling it upward. We measure the effects of black political empowerment by using the total number of black elected officials, as reported yearly by the Joint Center for Political and Economic Studies. Our analysis improves scale comparability by using a log of the actual number of black elected officials for each year between 1973 and 1994 rather than the raw number of black elected officials in a given year to estimate the impact of black empowerment on black political and organizational work.[3] Each quarter of aggregate civic activity is predicted by the logged number of black elected officials in the previous year. As we noted earlier, this allows us to capture the effects of the number of black elected officials in the same year that respondents reported their political activity.

JACKSON'S PRESIDENTIAL CANDIDACIES

We expect the Jackson presidential candidacies in 1984 and 1988 to pull black civic participation upward. We examine the separate effects of each of the Jackson campaigns because previous evidence suggests a surge and decline affect on black electoral participation where black political participation surged in 1984 and dipped in 1988 (Tate 1991). We create a binary code (1 = year of Jackson candidacy, 0 = other years) to assess the impact of Jackson's campaigns. Given the question wording in the Roper survey requiring respondents to catalog activities in the past year, we capture the effects of Jackson's campaigns in the same year as respondents' activity took place by coding the Jackson variable for the years 1985 and 1989.[4]

PARTY IN POWER

Our measure of the party in power is whether a Democrat holds the presidency (1 = Democrat, 0 = Republican). A Democrat in the White House should empower blacks to engage in civic activities because the party in power on the national level is perceived as positively predisposed to their policy preferences. The perception of accessibility and

[3] Rather than being measured in the thousands, BEOs are now measured on a metric that is similar to the other variables. See Appendix B for descriptive statistics.

[4] Respondents were not asked about their activities during 1984 and 1988 until 1985 and 1989, respectively.

the belief that party elites will be more responsive if the party preferred by a majority of blacks is in the White House would therefore push aggregate levels of black participation upward.

CHANGES IN BLACK COLLEGE ENROLLMENT

We consider aggregate-level educational advancement to be a macro-level indicator of political empowerment because the educational advancement of blacks as a group is reflected in the percentage of blacks entering higher education each year. As such, we expect that increases in black college enrollment will have a positive effect on black activism, pulling it upward. We estimate the effects of education as a collective resource using the rate of black college enrollment among high school graduates in each year. Because of survey question wording, college enrollment rates from the previous year are used to estimate participation in the following year.

MEASURES OF SOCIAL AND ECONOMIC DISTRESS

We are interested in whether macro-level social and economic distress measures may have pushed aggregate-level black political participation downward in the post–civil rights era. More than measures that tap whether blacks are making retrospective or prospective assessments of the economy, these indicators of economic and social conditions reflect the *consequences* of economic and social change in black communities. We consider five measures of economic and social distress: changes in economic disparities among blacks, changes in black unemployment, inflation, yearly immigration rates, and black criminal victimization rates.

Changes in Inequality Within the Black Population

We use a measure of income inequality among blacks – estimated by GINI coefficients – to assess whether rising inequality within black communities has influenced macro-level political participation. Again, we argue that the widening gap between the haves and the have-nots among blacks should pull macro-levels of black civic activity downward. GINI coefficients from the previous year are used to estimate participation in the following year.

Yearly Rates of Black Unemployment

We use black unemployment figures as a measure of economic distress. As the rates of black unemployment increase, we argue that aggregate levels of black participation should shift downward. The unemployment rate is the percentage of blacks that are unemployed in a given year. Black unemployment rates from the previous year are used to estimate participation in the following year.

Changes in the Inflation Rate

Another economic indicator of distress is the national rate of inflation (measured as the price-deflated gross domestic product). We argue that downward turns in the economy should pull aggregate levels of black participation downward. We use the change in price-deflated GDP from the previous year to estimate aggregate-level black participation in the following year.

Yearly Rate of Immigration

We see immigration as an indirect measure of social distress. We use yearly immigration rates to explore the economic consequences of immigration on black civic participation. We expect increases in immigration rates to push black civic activism downward. We use the percent change in the number of immigrants from the previous year to estimate participation in the following year.

Criminal Victimization Among Blacks

We use the percentage of blacks who have been victimized by crime as another indicator of social distress. We suggest that this measure is closely related to social decay in black communities, pulling aggregate levels of black civic participation downward. We use black victimization rates from the previous year to estimate participation in the following year.

ESTIMATING THE EFFECTS OF EMPOWERMENT AND DISTRESS

Given our theory of countervailing forces, we are primarily concerned with assessing the push-and-pull effects of our black empowerment and social and economic distress measures. Therefore, in this section, we primarily focus on discussing the relative effects of macro factors on changes in black civic participation. Tables 5.1 through 5.3 report unstandardized coefficients for our empowerment and distress measures. Here, we evaluate the effectiveness of our countervailing forces theory by calculating the expected change in value (EC) for each statistically significant variable in our models. This value allows us to compare the magnitude of the effects of selected variables relative to other variables in the models. For example, it allows us to ask: How much does black office-holding or inflation impact black activism during the time period under study?

Table 5.1 shows the results of our analysis of the push and pull of macro forces on black composite participation and across demographic groups. We report the expected change in value for statistically significant explanatory variables in each model in the columns labeled "EC." A comparison of the results for political empowerment relative to social and economic distress shows that black office-holding pulls black civic activism upward. It is interesting to note that when we consider the relative effects of empowerment and distress for blacks overall, black office-holding pulls black participation upward at about the same rate that income inequality pulls it downward. However, when we further consider the negative impact of immigration, we see that our distress measures swamp the overall positive influence of empowerment for this group. Even though we do not see the same pattern at work on the activism of black southerners, our results show that distress factors are devastating on the participation of black men, where most of our distress measures pull down their participation. Somewhat similar to our findings for blacks generally, social and economic distress factors also swamp the positive effects of the 1984 Jackson campaign on the civic activism of non-southerners. None of our political empowerment measures explain the composite participation of black women, and only one indicator of distress, immigration, explains their participation, pulling it downward.

TABLE 5.1. *GLS Models of Aggregate Black Composite Participation, 1973–1994*

Independent variables	Generalized Least Squares Coefficients (robust standard errors in parentheses)									
	All	EC[a]	South	EC	Non-South	EC	Male	EC	Female	EC
Political Empowerment										
Black elected officials	.43*		.63*		.29		.64**		.25	
	(.20)	.49	(.26)	.69	(.21)		(.21)	.73	(.23)	
Jackson 1984	.12		.05		.16+		.09		.15	
	(.08)		(.09)		(.09)	.16	(.07)		(.09)	
Jackson 1988	.09		−.04		−.16		.06		.11	
	(.07)		(.06)		(.11)		(.08)		(.08)	
Democratic presidency	−.06		−.07		−.09		−.03		−.09	
	(.05)		(.05)		(.08)		(.06)		(.06)	
College enrollment	−.01		−.00		−.01		−.01		−.01	
	(.01)		(.01)		(.01)		(.01)		(.01)	
Economic and Social Distress										
Black income inequality	−.05**		−.05		−.06**		−.06**		−.04	
	(.02)	.54	(.04)		(.01)	.59	(.02)	.67	(.03)	
Black unemployment	−.01		−.03*		.01		−.02+		−.01	
	(.01)		(.01)	.27	(.01)		(.01)	.18	(.01)	
Inflation rate	−.03		−.03		−.02		−.03**		−.03	
	(.02)		(.03)		(.02)		(.01)	.25	(.02)	
Immigration rate	−.05**		−.03		−.08**		−.06**		−.05**	
	(.01)	.28	(.02)		(.02)	.42	(.02)	.30	(.01)	.24
Criminal victimization	.01		.00		.01		.02*		.00	
	(.01)		(.02)		(.01)		(.01)	.27	(.01)	
Constant	−.18		−2.08*		1.25		−1.41		.99	
	(.90)		(.89)		(1.13)		(1.07)		(.96)	
Prob. > F	.00		.00		.00		.00		.00	
R^2	.47		.43		.61		.38		.47	
Number of cases	83		82[b]		83		83		83	

**$p < .01$, *$p < .05$ (two-tailed test), +$p < .10$ (one-tailed test)

[a] The expected change in value is reported for statistically significant explanatory variables in each model. Expected changes in value are calculated by multiplying the range of each variable of interest by its unstandardized coefficient.

[b] Data by region for the first two points in the survey (third and fourth quarters of 1973) is missing.

Source: Roper Trends data set, 1973–1994

Table 5.2 shows the effects of political empowerment and social and economic distress on aggregate-level political work. Recall that political work is an index of four participation acts: attending a rally or speech, being a member of a political party, being a member of a political organization, and signing a petition. The columns labeled "EC" in Table 5.2 show that the negative effects of growing income disparities within black communities directly countered the positive effects of black office-holding for the general black population and for black men. Compared to our results for composite participation, we see a similar push-and-pull pattern on black political work where our social and economic distress factors continue to swamp the positive benefits of our measures of political empowerment.

Although the 1988 Jackson campaign provides a boost to black political work for blacks in general, the additional weight of increasing inflation pushes black civic activism downward. For black men, we also see that economic and social distress measures considerably depress their activism. We find that college enrollment is negatively related to participation for this group. For black southerners, black office-holding pulls civic activism upward while immigration has a relatively small impact on pulling their activism down. Contrary to our expectations, a Democratic presidency does not empower black southerners' civic activism. And, similar to our findings for composite black participation, the activism of blacks outside of the South was more constrained by distress factors such as income inequality and immigration than boosted by the positive effects of Jackson's 1988 campaign. As in the models of composite participation, we find that immigration pushes the activism of black women downward, while our empowerment measures have little or negative effects on aggregate levels of their participation.

Table 5.3 shows the results of our models of black organizational work using our countervailing effects theory for all blacks and for blacks by region and by gender. Our theory of countervailing forces explains less variation across the models of aggregate organizational work than across the models of political work, as should be expected given the sporadic nature of black engagement in organizational work that we showed in Chapter 3. Organizational work may include activities as diverse as presiding over the social committee in a local group and attending a PTA meeting.

TABLE 5.2. *GLS Models of Aggregate Black Political Work, 1973–1994*

Independent Variables	Generalized Least Squares Coefficients (robust standard errors in parentheses)									
	All	EC[a]	South	EC	Non-South	EC	Male	EC	Female	EC
Political Empowerment										
Black elected officials	.20*		.28*		.12		.33**		.09	
	(.09)	.23	(.12)	.33	(.11)		(.10)	.37	(.09)	
Jackson 1984	.05		−.00		.07		.04		.06	
	(.04)		(.03)		(.05)		(.03)		(.04)	
Jackson 1988	.06+		−.02		.10+		.06		.05	
	(.03)	.06	(.03)		(.06)	.10	(.04)		(.04)	
Democratic presidency	−.03		−.05*		−.04		−.01		−.05*	
	(.03)		(.02)	.05	(.05)		(.03)		(.03)	.05
College enrollment	−.01		−.00		−.00		−.01*		−.00	
	(.00)		(.00)		(.01)		(.00)	.12	(.00)	
Economic and Social Distress										
Black income inequality	−.02**		−.02		−.03*		−.03**		−.01	
	(.01)	.23	(.02)		(.01)	.26	(.01)	.33	(.01)	
Black unemployment	−.00		−.01		.01		−.00		−.00	
	(.00)		(.01)		(.01)		(.00)		(.01)	
Inflation rate	−.02*		−.01		−.01		−.02**		−.01	
	(.01)	.12	(.01)		(.01)		(.01)	.14	(.01)	
Immigration rate	−.02**		−.02**		−.03**		−.02**		−.02**	
	(.01)	.12	(.01)	.09	(.01)	.16	(.01)	.12	(.01)	.11
Criminal victimization	.00		.00		.00		.01**		.00	
	(.01)		(.01)		(.01)		(.00)	.16	(.00)	
Constant	−.16		−1.18**		.68		−.83		.45	
	(.39)		(.40)		(.57)		(.51)		(.42)	
Prob. > F	.00		.00		.00		.00		.00	
R^2	.54		.58		.57		.46		.52	
Number of cases	83		82[b]		83		83		83	

$^{**}p < .01$, $^{*}p < .05$ (two-tailed test), $+p < .10$ (one-tailed test)

[a] The expected change in value is reported for statistically significant explanatory variables in each model. Expected changes in value are calculated by multiplying the range of each variable of interest by its unstandardized coefficient.

[b] Data by region for the first two points in the survey (third and fourth quarters of 1973) is missing.

Source: Roper Trends data set, 1973–1994

TABLE 5.3. *GLS Models of Aggregate Black Organizational Work, 1973–1994*

Independent Variables	Generalized Least Squares Coefficients (robust standard errors in parentheses)									
	All	EC[a]	South	EC	Non-South	EC	Male	EC	Female	EC
Political Empowerment										
Black elected officials	.19+		.28*		.12		.22+		.16	
	(.10)	.22	(.13)	.32	(.09)		(.12)	.25	(.12)	
Jackson 1984	.05		.04		.06		.05		.06	
	(.04)		(.05)		(.04)		(.04)		(.04)	
Jackson 1988	.02		−.03		.05		.02		.02	
	(.03)		(.04)		(.05)		(.04)		(.04)	
Democratic presidency	−.02		−.02		−.04		−.01		−.03	
	(.02)		(.03)		(.03)		(.03)		(.03)	
College enrollment	.00		−.00		−.00		−.00		−.00	
	(.00)		(.00)		(.00)		(.00)		(.00)	
Economic and Social Distress										
Black income inequality	−.03**		−.03		−.03**		−.02*		−.03*	
	(.01)	.28	(.02)		(.01)	.26	(.01)	.26	(.01)	.31
Black unemployment	−.00		−.01		−.00		−.01		−.00	
	(.01)		(.01)		(.01)		(.01)		(.01)	
Inflation rate	−.01		−.01		−.01		−.01		−.01	
	(.01)		(.01)		(.01)		(.11)		(.01)	
Immigration rate	−.02**		−.01		−.04**		−.03**		−.02**	
	(.01)	.12	(.31)		(.01)	.21	(.01)	.12	(.01)	.11
Criminal victimization	.00		.00		.00		.01*		−.00	
	(.01)		(.01)		(.00)		(.00)		(.01)	
Constant	.09		−.57		.56		−.25		.43	
	(.47)		(.46)		(.50)		(.60)		(.50)	
Prob. > *F*	.00		.00		.00		.00		.00	
R^2	.41		.07		.66		.33		.41	
Number of cases	83		82[b]		83		83		83	

$^{**}p < .01$, $^{*}p < .05$ (two-tailed test), $+p < .10$ (one-tailed test)

[a] The expected change in value is reported for statistically significant explanatory variables in each model. Expected changes in value are calculated by multiplying the range of each variable of interest by its unstandardized coefficient.

[b] Data by region for the first two points in the survey (third and fourth quarters of 1973) is missing.

Source: Roper Trends data wet, 1973–1994

The columns labeled "EC" in Table 5.3 report the expected values of the statistically significant explanatory variables in each of the organizational work models. Again, we see evidence of the countervailing effects of political empowerment and social and economic distress. The positive effects of black office-holding is swamped by the negative effects of income inequality and immigration rates. For black men, we see the same pattern. For non-southerners and black women, we see no benefits from our measures of political empowerment, and the consistently swamping effects of income inequality and immigration. In the South, increasing numbers of black elected officials had a positive effect on black organizational work that was not countered by any social or economic distress.

COUNTERVAILING EFFECTS ACROSS MODES OF PARTICIPATION

Our models indicate that political factors influence aggregate black participation in various modes of civic and political activity in a number of ways. Black office-holding results in greater levels of participation in political work, organizational work, and composite participation among blacks generally, and more specifically among southern blacks and black men. Jackson's more mainstream 1988 campaign had a positive effect on aggregate-level political work for blacks overall and for non-southern blacks. This finding makes intuitive sense when one considers the likely impact that Jackson had on mobilizing black candidates to compete for elective office, thereby not only increasing opportunities for blacks to attend political rallies for candidates, but also directly affecting the number of black elected officials in office.[5]

Despite contrary findings by other scholars, we find that the mobilizing influence of Jackson's campaigns generally did not have a significant effect during this period. Jackson's candidacies may have had time-bound effects that were only felt in the immediate aftermath of his campaigns. His second presidential campaign success apparently was strong enough to generate an effect on aggregate levels of political

[5] A cursory analysis of the impact of Jackson's candidacies on the numbers of black elected officials indicates a statistically significant and positive relationship that encourages our speculations about Jackson's indirect role in increasing black political participation. This result requires further study, however.

work for blacks overall and for non-southern blacks, but not for other demographic segments or organizational work during the time period under study.

As a measure of political empowerment, having a Democratic president has a consistently negative relationship with aggregate-level black activity across all of the models. Only for southern blacks' and black women's participation in political work does the relationship reach statistical significance. These results square well with Tate's (1993) finding that black turnout in 1984 and 1988 increased owing to a mixture of mobilization efforts from the Jackson campaigns and the political threat posed by policies of the Reagan administration. Perhaps rather than responding favorably to enhanced political accessibility, blacks are more motivated by the perception of political threat from the Republican Party.

Advances in college enrollment among blacks as a group do not result in increases in aggregate-level participation in political and organizational civic activities, nor in black composite participation, though there is a marginally significant negative effect in political work among black men. Although we expected that improving black educational attainment would increase black participation, these results are not particularly surprising given studies that show that increasing educational attainment over time in the United States has not led to overall increases in political participation more generally (Nie, Junn, and Stehlik-Barry 1996). As Norman Nie, Jane Junn, and Kenneth Stehlik-Barry (1996) demonstrate in their study of education and political participation, increases in formal education in the United States over the several decades has not lead to greater levels of political engagement. As they explain, "for political engagement, formal education works as a sorting mechanism, assigning ranks on the basis of the citizens' relative education attainment. Relative education is not the absolute number of years attained but the amount of education attained compared to those against whom the citizen competes" (1996, 6). Thus, as education levels in society improve, the impact of education on participation will vary depending on the degree to which others have obtained the same level of education. Therefore, increases in the number of blacks attending college might not have any affect on aggregate levels of black civic activism despite the tremendous gains that blacks have made in pursuing higher education.

Aggregate-level measures of social and economic distress add to our understanding of factors that have generally depressed black participation in civic activities. The immigration rate depresses black participation in all of the political work models and most of the organizational work and composite participation models. Based on our macro-level analysis of black civic participation, immigration has a consistently negative effect on black civic behavior during the time period under study. The economic consequences of rising immigration marginally depress black civic participation for all demographic groups and in all modes of civic activity except for organizational work among black southerners. The increased entry of low-skilled and semiskilled laborers into the workforce economically dislocates black workers, which may, in turn, leave blacks with fewer material resources to engage in civic activities beyond voting.

Although theoretically important, criminal victimization rates do not add much explanatory value to our models of aggregate-level participation in political and organizational work. The positive, statistically significant relationship between increased victimization and black men's aggregate level civic activities in each set of models is somewhat counterintuitive, especially given our expectations from research on the depressing effects of crime on civic participation in neighborhoods. It may be that increases in violent crime in the 1980s and 1990s have stimulated organizing activity to rid urban communities of crime (Patillo-McCoy 1999). High levels of victimization may increase aggregate levels of black civic participation by stimulating African Americans to contact their public officials, organize community groups to address problems, or rally their neighbors to respond to heightened levels of criminal activity.

Our study finds that economic disparity among blacks is negatively related to aggregate black political work, organizational work, and composite participation. Growing income inequality within the black population is a statistically significant determinant of black political work for blacks overall, and specifically for non-southern blacks and black men. A similar trend was evidenced for black organizational work and composite participation. The likelihood of participating in organizing activities such as making a speech or sitting on a committee declines among all demographic segments of the black community as income inequality increases. Inflation also has a negative effect on aggregate black civic activity across models. Sharp changes in the inflation rate have a statistically significant negative effect on political work and composite participation for blacks generally and for black males in particular at the aggregate level. As inflation rises, blacks, and black males in particular, are less likely to engage in activities such as formally joining political parties or other political organizations or attending rallies.

SOCIAL CLASS AND BLACK CIVIC ACTIVISM

The importance of class distinctions within the black community has been implicit throughout this book. The negative impact of social and economic distress shouldered by blacks is likely disproportionately borne on the shoulders of the most economically vulnerable. Here, we explicitly consider the effects of political empowerment, social distress, and economic distress on the composite participation of various social class groupings in black communities.[6]

We use aggregate levels of educational attainment as a proxy measure for social class. The aggregate measure of "lower status" is the quarterly average of respondents who reported attaining less than a 12th grade education. The aggregate measure of working class is the quarterly average of those who reported having received at least a 12th grade education. In addition, the aggregate measure of middle-class (and upper-middle-class) blacks is the quarterly average of those who reported having completed some postsecondary education. Owing to changes in question wording by the Roper Survey (see Appendix A), we are missing data from the first five years of the survey series (1973–7). This means that we are perhaps underestimating class implications that would be revealed only in the early, most active participatory years of the post–civil rights era. We recognize this as a limitation in the data, but we believe that our analysis of aggregate-level black activism in the context of growing social class distinctions among blacks adds additional leverage to our examination of the macro dynamics of black civic participation.

[6] We also ran models predicting black political and organizational work by social class groupings. The models performed quite poorly, and the results are not reported in the text.

Black poverty and unemployment have hovered around double that of whites for the duration of the post–civil rights period. There are more poor whites than blacks in sheer numbers (about twenty million whites compared to nine million blacks in 1997), but economic distress has a more devastating impact on black communities than among whites (Walton and Smith 2000). We consider the possibility that the factors contributing to political empowerment and social and economic distress in the black community may have specific effects on aggregate levels of participation depending on social class. We find that the push-and-pull effects of empowerment and distress do, indeed, affect aggregate participation levels differently depending on class.

Before discussing the results of our statistical analysis, we present aggregate trends in black composite participation by social class from 1978 through 1994 in Figure 5.8. That the black middle class engages in vastly higher aggregate levels of civic activism is immediately apparent. For most of the survey period, middle-class blacks engaged in two to three times as many political acts as working-class or lower-status blacks on average. Whereas aggregate-level black participation by the middle class hovered between 1.5 and 2 acts between the late 1970s and mid-1980s, aggregate-level participation by working-class blacks hovered around half an act and aggregate-level participation by lower-status blacks was lower still. Aggregate-level participation by blacks in each of the social classes increased, in some cases quite sharply, during the early 1980s, coinciding with Reagan's two presidential terms. Middle-class participation begins a sharp fall in the late 1980s and does not rebound for the duration of the study period. Participation among working-class and lower-status blacks remains low through the entire period, but it does not experience the sharp and lasting decline that is evidenced at the aggregate level among middle-class blacks.

Table 5.4 presents the results of our models of black composite participation by social class. The results of our analysis of black activism and social class present a mixed bag for our countervailing effects thesis. For starters, the positive benefits of political empowerment are not spread equally across social classes. In fact, we find a negative relationship between black electoral success and aggregate-level civic participation among blacks at the lower end of the class ladder while Jackson's 1984 candidacy has a positive impact. Predictably, two distress measures, unemployment and inflation, also negatively affect the

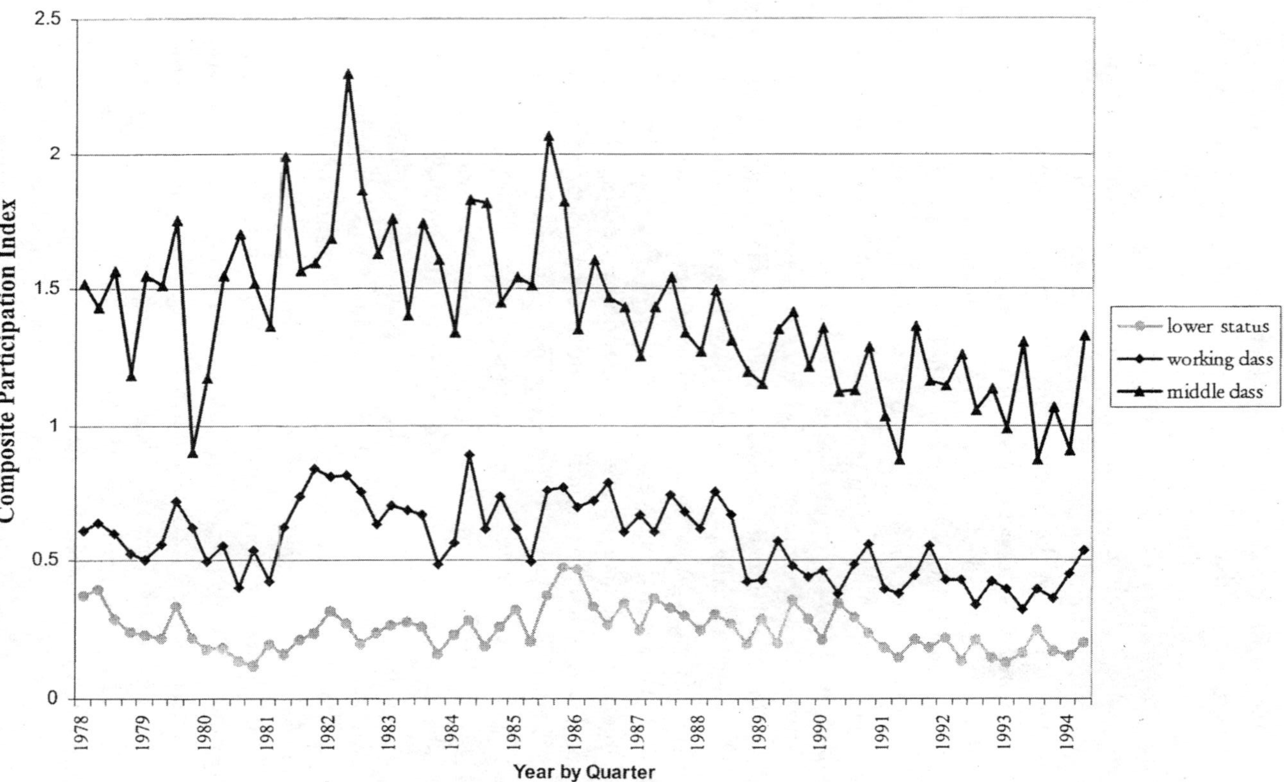

FIGURE 5.8. Composite participation index by social class, 1978–1999.

TABLE 5.4. *GLS Models of Aggregate Black Composite Participation, by Class, 1978–1994*

Independent Variables	Generalized Least Squares Coefficients (robust standard errors in parentheses)					
	Lower Status	EC[a]	Working Class	EC	Middle Class	EC
Political Empowerment						
Black elected officials	−.35+		−.46		.01	
	(.19)	.40	(.41)		(.58)	
Jackson 1984	.12*		.07		.26	
	(.06)	.12	(.07)		(.20)	
Jackson 1988	.04		.06		.36*	
	(.06)		(.09)		(.15)	.36
Democratic presidency	−.05		.11+		.03	
	(.03)		(.06)	.11	(.07)	
College enrollment	.00		−.01		−.03*	
	(.00)		(.01)		(.01)	.03
Economic and Social Distress						
Black income inequality	−.01		−.01		−.08	
	(.02)		(.03)		(.05)	
Black unemployment	−.01*		−.02		−.02	
	(.01)	.10	(.02)		(.03)	
Inflation rate	−.03*		−.03		−.06*	
	(.01)	.22	(.02)		(.03)	.43
Immigration rate	−.00		−.04*		−.05+	
	(.01)		(.01)	.23	(.03)	.27
Criminal victimization	.01		.02		.05*	
	(.01)		(.01)		(.02)	.76
Constant	3.85*		5.38*		5.03	
	(1.17)		(2.44)		(3.66)	
Prob. > F	.00		.00		.00	
R^2	.46		.58		.61	
Number of cases	66[b]		66		66	

$^{**}p < .01$, $^{*}p < .05$ (two-tailed test), $+p < .10$ (one-tailed test)

[a] The expected change in value is reported for statistically significant explanatory variables in each model. Expected changes in value are calculated by multiplying the range of each variable of interest by its unstandardized coefficient.

[b] Because of differences in question wording in the Roper Survey, data by class from 1973 through 1978 is missing.

Source: Roper Trends data set, 1973–1994

participation of lower-status blacks. Having a Democratic presidency has negative effects on the civic activism of working-class blacks, as does immigration. For middle-class blacks, the 1988 Jackson presidential campaign pulled the participation of this group forward, while two distress measures – immigration and inflation – pulled it downward. Interestingly, two of our indicators have effects that are opposite our expectations. College enrollment depresses the participation of middle-class blacks, while criminal victimization substantially increases middle-class civic activism.

The effects of these Jackson candidacies produce different effects across social class. Jackson's 1984 grassroots and 1988 traditional campaigns buoyed aggregate-level black composite participation for blacks at the low and high ends of the class spectrum. This suggests a potential tension between insurgent and traditional campaign strategies beyond an emphasis on Jackson's candidacies. It may well be that grassroots strategies serve to push participation among lower-status blacks upward, while having no effect on the participation levels of other blacks. Likewise, campaigns that emphasize traditional political strategies may energize aggregate levels of participation among middle-class blacks, while leaving lower-status blacks unmoved.

Aggregate-level participation among blacks is pushed downward by macro-level social and economic conditions across social classes. Our results indicate that middle- and upper-class blacks are grappling with the negative impact of inflation. We also see negative results from increasing immigration rates during the post–civil rights era. High black unemployment and increasing inflation depress aggregate-level composite participation among lower-status blacks, essentially demobilizing the most vulnerable blacks when they could be petitioning the government for more jobs, better pay, and enhanced unemployment benefits.

COUNTERVAILING FORCES ACROSS DEMOGRAPHIC GROUPS

In this section, we more closely examine the tug-of-war between political empowerment factors and social and economic distress factors across demographic groups. Because we observe different effects across our models, here we provide a fuller explanation of our findings. Our results demonstrate that the push-and-pull effects of empowerment and distress behave differently across region, gender, and social class.

Different factors explain changes in aggregate-level black activism in political work, organizational work, and composite participation depending on the region where blacks reside. Our models show that black office-holding was the most important factor pulling up the aggregate-level activism of southern blacks although black office-holding was not as relevant for aggregate activism in other areas of the country. The increase in black elected officials increased aggregate-level composite participation by more than one half an act and was the only variable to reach statistical significance in the model explaining southern organizational work. In the South, black gains in office-holding may signal a more welcoming political opportunity structure that galvanizes engagement in civic activity. Clearly, these findings attest to the critical role that the Voting Rights Act has had on the nonvoting civic activism of southern blacks. As blacks gain seats in city councils, school boards, and state legislatures, southern blacks may be more inclined to serve in parent–teacher associations, join neighborhood community watch organizations, or participate in petition drives.

Non-southern blacks were more responsive to Jesse Jackson's candidacies than to other political empowerment factors in our models. His 1984 campaign pulled aggregate-level composite participation for non-Southerners upward, while his 1988 campaign also pulled up aggregate levels of political work among blacks outside of the South. Black income inequality was a consistent retardant of civic participation for black non-Southerners. Increasing rates of immigration also had consistently negative effects on non-southern black civic activism. While immigration pushed aggregate-level civic activism downward across regions, the one–two punch of economic displacement and income disparity was especially detrimental for levels of non-southern black activism because political factors had little or no positive benefit.

Our models reveal much more about the factors informing changes in aggregate-level activism of black men than black women. For black men, BEOs were the dominant factor pulling their aggregate-level activism upward during the post–civil rights era. The effects were greatest for aggregate-level changes in black composite participation where BEOs contributed to nearly a three-quarter act increase in black male civic activism during the twenty-one years under study. Interestingly, criminal victimization was a robust predictor of increases in civic activism at the macro level for black men. This is the only segment of the population for which we find this result. Black men apparently respond to victimization in their communities by becoming more engaged in civic participation rather than less. The growing membership of black civic groups organized around black men's efforts to stem the tide of increased levels of crime in inner-city communities, such as MAD DADS (Men Against Destruction Defending Against Drugs and Social Disorder) is indicative of this aggregate-level response (Bingham 1991; *Los Angeles Times* 1995).

None of the political empowerment factors in our models worked as expected for black women. Immigration rates pushed aggregate-level activism downward for both black men and black women. In fact, immigration was the most consistent predictor across all of the models and the only variable that was significant in the model explaining the composite political activism of black women. The answer for why this is so may lie in black women's economic vulnerability. Historically, black women's work opportunities were dictated by racial and gender segmentation that kept them bound to agricultural and domestic work in the South and domestic work and limited manufacturing jobs in northern industry (Collins 2000, 57). Employment opportunities that afforded some black women less grueling work and more stable, middle-class incomes became more accessible in the post–World War II economy, but the economic vulnerability reinforced by intersecting racist and sexist institutions remained across class lines. Black women's economic uncertainty is further compounded by stagnant and declining job prospects in black communities more generally as a consequence of double-digit unemployment, repressive criminal justice programs, punitive social welfare policies, and global economic restructuring (Collins 2000). Many working-class and poor black women evince their civic activism in an environment of shrinking opportunities, and middle-class black women are not immune to the vagaries of economic fortune that allow some African Americans to get by, but not ahead (Collins 2000; Klein 2004).

However, micro-level factors such as the combined feelings of gender and race consciousness might be more relevant to black women's political activism than macro-level forces, which, in our models, substantially influence the political activism of black men but have hardly any effect on black women's political activism. The predominance of micro forces on black women's political activism is plausible given the importance of the intersectionality of race, class, and gender in the political life of black women (Giddings 1984; Gay and Tate 1998; Collins 2000).

Our models of composite participation by social class show that aggregate-level changes in the civic activism of lower-status, working-class, and middle-class blacks are pushed and pulled by different sets of macro-level factors. Two results require further elaboration here: the depressing effect of black electoral success on lower-status blacks and the positive effect of Jackson's 1988 candidacy on middle-class blacks.

Many students of black politics have argued that the primary beneficiaries of black political advancement have been middle- and upper-class blacks (Dawson 1994a; Gaines 1996; West 2001). Adolph Reed (1999) presents a scathing critique of the role of black elected officials from school superintendents to mayors to congressmen as modern-day "race managers" in the decades since the midcentury civil rights movement. Early connections between black elected officials and radical black nationalists notwithstanding, Reed argues that the incremental policy changes introduced by black politicians, their vested interests (by way of membership) in the very systems that require fundamental restructuring, and their ability through the use of superior resources to define the reasonable limits of political expectation have, along with other dynamics, "exerted a demobilizing effect on black politics" (1999, 121). Incumbent black politicians have very little incentive to encourage the political uncertainty that would likely result from the widespread mobilization of wide segments of the black community in electoral or protest politics. According to this view, after gaining entry into the reigning political order, black politicians shift to "politics as usual" to maintain their seats, increase their share of power, and deliver resources to constituencies that reliably support them at the polls. The negative relationship between the swelling ranks of black officials and lower-status participation (and, indeed, the worsening conditions of lower-status blacks across a range of indicators including poverty, education, and health care) prompts scholars to revisit "the uneven class-benefits" of black incorporation and the "demise of the 'black revolution'" (Johnson 2004).

Jackson's presidential candidacies also had varying effects across social classes. Lorn Foster argues that Jackson's initial presidential bid is best understood as "an extension of the civil rights movement," in that it was "organized more like a movement than a campaign" and derived its structure "more from the black church than from electoral politics" (1990, 203). The goals of the 1984 Jackson campaign were aimed at political empowerment by increasing black voter registration, encouraging and assisting blacks running for political office, and creating an electoral infrastructure in the black community (Cavanaugh and Foster 1984). Hence, Jackson's 1984 campaign is often characterized as an effort to champion the cause of the black poor. The positive effect of Jackson's first presidential run on the civic participation of lower-status blacks can be explained by the more insurgent focus of his first campaign.

By contrast, Robert Smith (1990) criticizes Jackson's 1988 campaign for abandoning its insurgent roots in favor of traditional Democratic Party politics. Recall that Jackson's 1988 compaign increased aggregate-level activism of middle-class, but not lower- or working-class, blacks. Reed argues that Jackson's shift in strategy in 1988 was "crafted to project his image as a responsible insider" and gain him "quasi-official status in the Democratic hierarchy" (1999, 144–5). The unintended consequence of Jackson's second presidential campaign, according to Reed, was that it "demobilized blacks' participation in the debate over the party's future... demobilized black Democrats by defining their interests solely in relation to Jackson's personal fortunes," and facilitated the burgeoning rightward move of the Democratic Leadership Council in the Democratic Party (1999, 144–9). Our results suggest that even though Jackson's second presidential campaign might not have spurred civic activism among all blacks, it did have a positive effect on the participation of middle-class blacks.

As the class divide in black America expands and poverty becomes more concentrated in the inner-cities where political, economic, and social resources are fewer and interaction across class lines is less frequent, opportunities for resource sharing between middle-class and lower-class blacks become more limited thus compounding social isolation. Declining civic participation among blacks overall is likely only one consequence among many. Lower-status blacks may be increasingly isolated from the mobilizing efforts of political candidates, political parties, and interest groups.

In conclusion, our analysis of the effects of empowerment and distress on aggregate levels of civic participation for blacks overall, as well as across regions and gender provides strong evidence for our countervailing forces theory. While the push and pull of empowerment and distress on black civic activism varies across the type of activity – composite participation, political work, and organizational work – as well as across demographic groups, we find that our measures of macro-level distress factors consistently swamp the benefits gained from our measures of black empowerment over the course of twenty-one years. These findings have implications for understanding the effects of structural barriers on black civic participation in the post–civil rights era. We discuss these implications, among others, in the concluding chapter.

6

From Margin to Center

Bringing Structural Forces into Focus in the Analysis of Black Activism

> A community is democratic only when the humblest and weakest person can enjoy the highest civil, economic, and social rights that the biggest and most powerful possess.
>
> A. Philip Randolph

Our findings in this study pose a question that is at the heart of the debate about the state of black political life at the turn of the twenty-first century – can black political equality be accomplished without economic equality? We assess the state of political equality for African Americans since the civil rights movement by exploring how two competing forces – black political empowerment and social and economic distress – influence civic participation in black communities. Exploring fluctuations in black activism over the course of the first two and a half decades after the 1960s civil rights revolution, our study demonstrates that black civic life has exhibited a tug-of-war between the empowering effects of black office-holding on the one hand and the stagnating effects of social and economic distress on the other. The primacy of distress in the tug-of-war between empowerment and economic factors is an unanticipated outcome from the civil rights movement's focus on the guarantee of formal political rights in the transition from protest to the promise of blacks' equal access in mainstream political life.

The movement and the landmark legal reforms that emerged in response to mass action altered the American political landscape by opening opportunities for blacks to have their voices heard equally as civic actors in mainstream political life. During the late 1960s and early 1970s, the nation experienced a "participation revolution" (Milbrath and Goel 1977, 144). Groups that had previously been excluded from mainstream politics utilized innovative, unconventional means to demand that they be treated as "political equals" (Dahl 1971). African Americans, followed by women, students, and other excluded or marginal groups, challenged American political institutions to open the channels of communication so that they could voice their preferences before political decision makers in an equal contest with other competing groups, thereby opening up a larger place for themselves in the political system.

The movement's incorporation into American politics offered political access and influence that had not existed for blacks since the end of Reconstruction. With the election of black public officials, active participation in Democratic Party politics, and the fielding of a viable black presidential candidate, African Americans' participation in the civic life of the nation was thought to give strength to voices that were once marginal.

The success of the civil rights movement highlighted by the triumphant passage of the 1964 Civil Rights Act and the 1965 Voting Rights Act cemented what has been coined the "Second Reconstruction" for black Americans (Woodward [1966] 1974; Marshall 1987; Kousser 1999). With the passage of the 1965 Voting Rights Act, "[a] new American constitution came into being, with African Americans more fully integrated into the mainstream of the nation's social, economic, and political life" (Riley 1999, 264). The results of this new legal access for blacks were swift and enduring. White politicians, especially Southerners and presidential contenders, could no longer safely ignore the growing numbers of black voters. The overt racially degrading rhetoric of white segregationists was muted for the foreseeable future, and a new climate of racial tolerance emerged (Tate 1993, 167).

Black protest pressed forward to organize effective strategies in this new political landscape with the ballot as the central tactical weapon of the emerging struggle and black office-holding as the key to greater empowerment in the political system. The protest tactics of the civil rights movement had successfully secured basic civil rights for African Americans and for the first time since Reconstruction, the black electorate was "nationalized," with mounting increases in black voter registration and turnout in the South expanding the political opportunities of blacks in politics. As a consequence of government repression against civil rights and black power organizations and the internal disputes and competition between civil rights organizations, large-scale protest as a viable political alternative in black communities was subordinated in favor of channeling of community resources into electoral politics. This transition took place with ease since the push for voting rights and the election of blacks to public office had been a major platform in the civil rights movement agenda. Indeed, securing voting rights and establishing voter registration and citizenship schools to prepare southern blacks for voter requirements were key objectives of mainstream civil rights organizations such as the Southern Christian Leadership Conference (SCLC) as well as radical groups like the Black Panthers.

As the civil rights movement declined, leadership nurtured in protest organizations began to see mainstream politics as a new venue for advocating on behalf of black communities. Former movement activists ran for public office during the 1970s, 1980s, and into the 1990s, facilitating the transition from protest activism to electoral politics. SCLC activist Andrew Young served three terms in the U.S. Congress, was appointed United Nations Ambassador, and served two terms as mayor of Atlanta. Student Nonviolent Coordinating Committee (SNCC) activists Marion Barry and Eleanor Holmes Norton also pursued careers in public office with Barry using organizing skills honed during the movement to mobilize poor and working-class blacks in support of his first successful mayoral bids in Washington, D.C., and Norton winning a congressional seat as the District's representative. John Lewis, once the National Director of SNCC, won office as a U.S. Representative from Georgia, and former Black Panther Bobby Rush was elected to Congress from Chicago's South Side.

Our findings indicate that the transition from protest to electorally oriented politics had empowering effects on black civic life after the 1960s. Although the impact of black empowerment on civic life varies across demographic groups and by the type of civic activity, the presence of black elected officials increases black civic participation in the aggregate black population. Specifically, when assessing the tug-of-war between the forces of empowerment and distress across a spectrum of political activities, black office-holding pulls aggregate levels of activism upward. And when assessing the effects for black Southerners engaged in activities such as working in political campaigns and attending political rallies, the relative effects of black office-holding on participation is even stronger. As scholars have documented in previous studies, and as our findings confirm, black office-holding matters for black civic participation.

But the empowering effects of black empowerment tell only part of the story of black civic life since the movement. In the tug-of-war between the two opposing forces, black civic life has been significantly muted by social and economic realities that have confronted black communities in the first decades after the 1960s. Our analysis shows that growing income inequality within the black population; rising prices in goods, services, and production; and surges in immigration depress bundles of black civic activities in the general black population. When we simultaneously assess the positive effects of black office-holding with the negative effects of distress, we find that these two forces compete against the other in explaining black civic activism.

Our findings are clear for three types of black civic activities (composite, political work, and organizational involvement): The positive participatory benefits of black office-holding in the post–civil rights era are swamped by the negative forces of income inequality, inflation, and immigration for blacks across the nation. The swamping effects of economic distress restructure the activities that allow African Americans to communicate their political voices directly in the polity by attending political rallies, working for political parties, and being members of organizations interested in better government. Thus, despite the positive signals that black elected officials give to encourage civic participation in the black population, the corrosive forces of economic distress weaken the political voices of African Americans in their quest to express their concerns beyond the voting booth.

UNDERSTANDING THE DYNAMICS OF AFRICAN-AMERICAN ACTIVISM

We return to the fictional families we introduced at the beginning of our study – the Jeffersons and the Evanses. The different circumstances they faced over the course of their lives highlight how changing circumstances in the political, social, and economic environment are pivotal to understanding the dynamics of black civic life in the post–civil rights era. Although each of the individuals in the families possesses assorted levels of resources in the form of education, income, and occupational status and has different levels of civic engagement, when we aggregate their total activism, the distinctions smooth out and a new story emerges. When we look at the combined activities of the Evanses and the Jeffersons at the aggregate level, our theory of countervailing forces would show that despite the positive effects of black office-holding in stimulating their activism as a group, negative economic forces constrain their collective participatory output regardless of their individual capacity to engage in civic activities. The story of the fictional Jeffersons and Evanses emerges in reality in contemporary black life.

In the first-ever longitudinal study assessing black civic participation in the post–civil rights era, our work makes both theoretical and analytical contributions to the study of black participation. We demonstrate that black civic activism is dynamic, not static. Aggregate levels of activism respond to social, economic, and political forces in the environment that create barriers to and opportunities for black civic activity. As we pointed out in our historical survey of black civic participation prior to the civil rights movement in Chapter 4, the push-and-pull characteristics of black civic participation provide a framework for unraveling the dynamics of black civic participation over time. We develop a framework that incorporates blacks' pursuit of political empowerment *and* the economic and social realities of black life. We isolate the net result of this tug-of-war between empowerment on the one hand and socioeconomic realities on the other across time and demographic groups, building on research that has previously only examined empowerment and economic issues separately.

Our theory proposes that empowerment and distress factors could balance each other in influence, creating a kind of equilibrium where black civic engagement plateaus for a period of time, neither increasing nor declining in response to macro factors. In a context characterized by escalating immigration, high inflation, and high income inequality, our theory would predict a decline in black activism as blacks adjust to decreases in the material resources required to engage in political and organizational activities. Alternatively, in a period characterized by black electoral success, strong national black candidacies, and moderate to low immigration, inflation, and black unemployment, our theory would predict a stronger pull from empowerment factors pulling black civic activism higher.

From an analytical perspective, our approach to understanding black civic participation in aggregate terms helps us to uncover macro forces that bear on black civic life and to build a profile of black civic life over time. We achieve these improvements by shifting the level of analysis up from the individual level to examine aggregate levels of black civic activity, by bringing structure (here defined as macro-level political, social, and economic forces) into the analysis of black political behavior, and by employing data that tracks black civic activism over twenty-one years.

These methodological advancements allow us to remedy the theoretical and inferential mismatch so prevalent in models of black political behavior that claim to explain group behavior through the analysis of cross-sectional individual-level data. The wealth of research on black participation shares our intuition that black participation is a collective phenomena; however, most of these studies draw inferences about the experiences of "black America," "the black community," or "the black electorate," from individual-level analysis. With the exception of a handful of aggregate-level analyses, these studies draw conclusions about blacks as a group without measuring group behavior.

The most important works to date on black partisanship (Gurin, Hachett, and Jackson 1989), political attitudes (Dawson 1994a), voting behavior (Tate 1994), and group-based resources (Cohen and Dawson 1989; Harris 1999a) are based on cross-sectional studies with large black samples but only two or three data points to compare over time. These studies provide only a glimpse at black political behavior in a given moment in time. In our approach, we capture the dynamic nature of black civic engagement because our longitudinal approach allows us to model fluctuations in black activism over time. Historical analysis guided our claims and our statistical analyses confirmed our intuition that macro-level exogenous forces shape macro-level political behavior. Never holding a stationary pattern over time, our results demonstrate that average black civic activism rises and falls in response to macro-level changes in black political, social, and economic fortunes.

Our dynamic approach to black behavior has implications for understanding the micro dynamics of black political participation. Individual decisions to participate in the political process may be conditioned on macro-level factors, where less distress in the economic environment may provide incentives for blacks to become civically active while greater distress may provide disincentives for participation. Macro-level social, economic, and, to a lesser extent, political forces fluctuate, which might affect individual-level decisions to engage in civic and political activities. For any individual citizen, growing levels of social and economic distress would place greater costs on political participation than would be the case during periods of good economic times.

Although our macro approach has implications for understanding individual decisions to participate in civic activities, there are individual or micro dynamics in black political behavior that cannot be accounted for in our approach. Our macro approach, while improving the inferences that can be made about black behavior as group behavior, obscures micro-level processes that are important to black civic life in general and black participation in particular. We know through the work of Bobo and Gilliam (1990) that black empowerment increases black civic participation through enhanced feelings of political efficacy and trust in the political system. Other scholars have noted the importance of group consciousness in stimulating black participation (Shingles 1981). These are micro dynamics that foster black participation and do not easily translate into the macro world.

We also recognize how important ideology and issue preferences are for stimulating black participation. Our macro approach, for instance, does not allow us to examine group solidarity and how it motivates individuals in black communities to engage in political action. An individual's participation could be influenced by a commitment to egalitarian ideas about racial justice or a commitment to ideas of black solidarity rooted in Black Nationalist traditions. Because personal commitments to ideas may shift over time and because of the lack of longitudinal data on blacks' ideological preferences, we cannot specify the individual motivations (nor aggregate motivations of blacks as a group) that drive black civic participation over the period of our analysis. Similarly, we do not know what issues are motivating individual actors in black communities at particular points in time. The actors in our surveys could be spurred into action by personal, local, or national issues. Activism evolving from national campaigns like the Anti-Apartheid Movement and the crusade for a national holiday for

Martin Luther King to local issues like police brutality or environmental racism are issue-driven episodes. Occurrences such as these more than likely motivated activism over the period of our study, but they cannot be accounted for in our model of black activism.

Despite some limitations to our approach, we have demonstrated that black participation is dynamic, responding to the macro-level political, social, and economic environment. We have presented a macro-level approach that is an alternative approach to thinking about black civic participation. So what do we think is the bottom line? Basically, we think that the research questions one pursues should dictate the use of a macro- or micro-level approach. We recognize that there are trade-offs to be made when pursuing a macro approach, but our study demonstrates that there is also much to be gained.

THE COMPLEXITIES OF EMPOWERMENT AND ACTIVISM

The contradiction of empowerment in the midst of social and economic setbacks has been an ongoing debate since black public officials began to win increasingly more elective offices in the 1970s. We argue that, unlike approaches to black behavior found in individual-level models, our aggregate-level measurement of empowerment positively predicts black activism, not because of its effect on attitudes but because black office-holding may send a bundle of signals to blacks about receptivity or threat in the political environment. As the number of blacks in elected office increases, blacks might interpret the presence of black elected officials as a signal of increased openness in the political sphere and respond by becoming more civically and politically active. However, despite the signaling mechanism that stimulates activism, commentators and scholars have questioned whether openness in the system has or can improve the material conditions of African Americans.

Writing during a period when the number of black elected officials was quickly accelerating, political activist Hoyt Fuller wondered in 1975 whether the over 3,500 black elected officials could bring any substantial change in tackling black inequality. In an appropriately titled essay, "Political Motion and the Static Black Condition," Fuller noted that "whatever benefits had accrued as a consequence of the added number of Black Elected Officials (BEO) were plainly recognizable only by the BEO's themselves. It is sadly ironic that, on every notable front, the state of well-being of ordinary Black people diminishes at the same rate as the number of BEOs increases" (1975, 49). Fuller saw these black elected officials reflecting the interest of the black middle class, operating as "achievers" fighting racism through the political system but primarily on behalf of "lifting the barriers of their own class" (1975, 86).

Several scholars point to the apparent inability or unwillingness of black elected officials to reverse significantly deteriorating material conditions for many blacks (Swain 1993; Smith 1996). Others suggest that black electoral success strategies are ill-equipped to pursue a radically transformative social justice agenda (Guinier 1994) and that black elected officials' realigned loyalties to political institutions and corporate interests might directly undermine such goals (Piven and Cloward 1979, 252–8). William Nelson's criticism of black mayors, "[e]lected on reform platforms that promised profound changes in the policy-making process," highlights the class bias in policies that have been "modestly successful in increasing access to public resources by members of the black middle class," while "virtually preclud[ing] the redistribution of major benefits to broad segments of the black community" (1987, 174).

Adolph Reed makes one of the strongest criticisms of black elected officials, calling them "race managers," whose desire to maintain their incumbency and power in office gives them incentive to "constrict the field of political discourse" and limit "the number and range of claims on the policy agenda" (1999, 121). In our empirical model testing the countervailing forces of the civic participation of the black poor in Chapter 5, we found an unexpected finding that further highlights the contradictions of empowerment and activism. In addition to the debilitating economic distress factors that depressed the civic participation of poor blacks, black office-holding also depressed the participation of poor blacks over time. Apparently, civic activism amongst the black poor has not been positively influenced by the presence of blacks in the political system, suggesting that the black poor have been demobilized and, as a consequence, have not benefited from the participatory benefits of black incorporation in the polity. This finding suggests that the positive signals that the presence of black elected officials sends encourage black civic participation in the general population but either are not disseminated to or are not seen as legitimate by the black poor. Over the course of the period under study here, the only empowerment factor that increased the participation of the black poor was Jesse Jackson's grassroots candidacy in 1984.

With the exception of our findings for less affluent blacks, critics of the black empowerment thesis should consider how structural forces in the American economy create barriers to black civic engagement. Again, our findings show that the participatory benefits that have accrued from black office-holding have been swamped by economic structural forces such as rising inequality, surges in prices for goods and services, and economic competition from immigration. Moreover, critics and black elected officials themselves often do not recognize that structural forces in the economy rather than the capacity of black elected officials to gain economic benefits for black communities through political institutions are responsible for the economic setbacks that African Americans have experienced in the post–civil rights era. Even with the many shortcomings of black empowerment strategies, based on our analysis, there is no question that blacks are better off with the limited gains in participation from black office-holding than they would be in the absence of empowerment politics. In the absence of the empowering effects of black electoral success, our theory of countervailing forces suggests that black civic engagement would have plummeted even farther. Black empowerment politics provides blacks with at least a glimmer of hope that their engagement in the American political system will be rewarded.

IMPLICATIONS FOR THE STUDY OF PARTICIPATION IN AMERICA

Though this study centers on the civic participation of African Americans and how empowerment and distress influence fluctuations in black activism over time, our findings have implications for understanding participation throughout American life. Here we briefly discuss the implications of our finding for understanding the dynamics of political participation in the United States. Even though longitudinal studies have uncovered trends in American civic and political participation (Rosenstone and Hansen 1993; Putnam 2000), few studies have systematically investigated how economic structural forces contribute to changes in American political participation over time. In Robert Putnam's analysis of declining civic engagement in the United States, he discussed several factors that may have eroded participation in civic organizations and political activities, citing pressures on time and the lack of money, suburbanization, generational change, and the advent of televisions as major sources of civic erosion (Putnam 2000, 284). Apart from a brief discussion of the possible effects of globalization on American civic life, structural economic forces such as fluctuations in unemployment or rising income inequality do not figure prominently in Putnam's explanation of why civic participation has experienced decline since the 1960s.

Indeed, with one notable exception – Schlozman and Verba's largely overlooked study of the effects of unemployment on participation (1979) – discussions of how forces in the American economy affect political participation have been at the margins of the study of American politics. The socioeconomic status model of political participation has dominated the field for more than a generation and scholars have documented time and time again "how the social status of an individual – his job, education, and income – determines a large extent how he participates" (Verba and Nie 1972, 13).

The conclusion drawn from the SES model is that citizens who lack individual resources are less likely to participate in the political process. Even though education, income, and occupational status are important individual predictors of participation, participation studies say little about how structural forces bear on the *capacity* of citizens – particularly economically marginal citizens – to foster and sustain personal resources for participation. By taking a macro approach to longitudinal studies that consider macro forces in the American economy such as income inequality, inflation, and unemployment, scholars in the field of political participation might discover and uncover patterns in participation that have been obscured by a focus on explaining individual capacities to participate in public life.

COUNTERVAILING FORCES AND NEW BARRIERS TO BLACK CIVIC LIFE

Even though there were political and legal barriers to black civic participation prior to the civil rights movement, our findings suggest that economic forces in the post–civil rights era have produced new barriers to securing black political equality. White supremacist violence, the abandonment of political parities, and legal restrictions constrained aspects of black civic participation in by-gone days; however, in the post–civil rights era, structural forces such as inflation, growing inequality, and the economic consequences of immigration appear to be undermining the legal gains of the civil rights movement and the political gains of black empowerment in the post–civil rights era as blacks continue to press for political equality.

A report from the American Political Science Association's Task Force on Political Inequality documents rising inequality in American life and asks what rising inequality means for the political equality of minority groups. "When less advantaged Americans experience stagnating economic fortunes and continuing disparities in political voice," the report notes, "the promise of greater equality for minorities is compromised" (American Political Science Association Task Force Report 2004, 661).

As the findings from our study suggest, the political voices of African Americans are weakened by forces beyond their control. The idea that political opportunities are recast as the social and economic fortunes of the nation is brought into focus in the context of our theory of countervailing forces. Although legal barriers to black participation have largely been removed, and though no politician consciously orchestrates high unemployment or rising prices to deliberately stymie black participation, the net result of countervailing structural effects is that blacks as a group disproportionately shoulder the brunt of social and economic woes and only marginally share in the rewards of social and economic good times. Our study reveals that political equality in the absence of economic equality may be an elusive goal for all African Americans, but particularly for poor African Americans whose levels of participation in civic life have not been activated by the presence of black elected officials.

If all sectors of society are to be addressed adequately in the public agenda of government, it is essential that participation occurs from diverse sectors of society (Milbrath and Goel 1977). Those Americans holding positions of privilege in public discourse and decision-making will find it difficult to maintain the allegiance of those who, for a variety of reasons, find their participatory opportunities systematically diminished by social, political, and economic forces beyond their control. More than a generation ago, President Lyndon Johnson observed during the civil rights movement that blacks were seeking more than the legal guarantee of unhindered access to the ballot booth. In a speech given after signing the Voting Rights Act of 1965, Johnson noted that blacks sought participation in the American political system with the ultimate goal of "secur[ing] for themselves the full blessings of American life" (see Riley 1999, 233).

The future of black civic life is cloudy as African Americans enter a new century of struggle. The viability of African-American civic life lies in the uncertainty of social and economic fortune. Indeed growing levels of inequality among blacks, between blacks and whites, and between working-class Americans and wealthy Americans suggest that civic life throughout American society may be in crisis. W. E. B. DuBois proclaimed that the problem of the twentieth century would be the "color line." Troubling trends in the economic and social conditions of African Americans – and for other minorities and the poor – suggest that barriers to economic equality may well be the most daunting problem in the twenty-first century as blacks continue to press for full political equality in American life.

Appendix A

Question Wording and Coding

DEPENDENT VARIABLES

Political Activity Series

Our survey data is from the Roper Social and Political Trends Data, 1973–1994. The following questions were asked regularly every year between 1973 and 1994:

Now here is a list of things some people do about government or politics. (HAND RESPONDENT CARD) Have you happened to have done any of those things in the past year? (IF "YES") Which ones?

CONTACT	Written your congressman or senator (1 = Yes, 0 = No)
ATTRALLY	Attended a political rally or speech (1 = Yes, 0 = No)
PUBMTG	Attended a public meeting on town or school affairs (1 = Yes, 0 = No)
OFFICE	Held or run for political office (1 = Yes, 0 = No)
ORGCMTE	Served on a committee for some local organization (1 = Yes, 0 = No)
ORGOFCR	Become (or served as) an officer of some club or organization (1 = Yes, 0 = No)
LETTER	Written a letter to the paper (1 = Yes, 0 = No)
PETITION	Signed a petition (1 = Yes, 0 = No)
PARTYWRK	Worked for a political party (1 = Yes, 0 = No)
SPEECH	Made a speech (1 = Yes, 0 = No)
ARTICLE	Written an article for a magazine or newspaper (1 = Yes, 0 = No)

ORGMBR Been a member of some group like the League of Women Voters or some other group interested in better government (1 = Yes, 0 = No)

Political Work

A quarterly additive index of the following four political activities:

Attended a political rally or speech
Worked for a political party
Been a member of a group interested in better government
Signed a petition

Organizational Work

A quarterly additive index of the following four civic activities:

Become or served as an officer of club or organization
Served on a committee for local organization
Made a speech
Attended a public meeting

Composite Participation Index

A quarterly additive index of the following for political and civic activities:

Written your congressman or senator
Attended a political rally or speech
Attended a public meeting on town or school affairs
Held or run for political office
Served on a committee for some local organization
Become (or served as) an officer of some club or organization
Written a letter to the paper
Signed a petition
Worked for a political party
Made a speech
Written an article for a magazine or newspaper
Been a member of some group like the League of Women Voters or some other group interested in better government

Demographic Coding

We analyzed the dependent variables in subsamples based on region (South, non-South), gender (male, female), and social class (lower status, working, middle/upper). The variables and coding used to create the subsamples are described next.

Region. Respondent's state of residence. No interviews were conducted in Alaska or Hawaii.

South	The eleven Old Confederacy states: Alabama, Arkansas, Georgia, Florida, Louisiana, Mississippi, North Carolina, South Carolina, Tennessee, Texas, Virginia.
Non-South	Mainland states outside of the south.

Gender. Respondent's sex. Coded by the interviewer (respondent was not asked this question).

1 Male
2 Female

Social Class. Respondent's Level of Education.
What was the last grade or regular school that you completed – not counting specialized schools like secretarial, art, or trade schools? (1978–1994)

1 No school
2 0–8
3 9–11
4 12
5 13–15
6 16
7 17+

Lower status (1–3) – Less than twelfth-grade education
Working class (4) – Twelfth-grade education
Middle/upper middle class (5–7) – Greater than twelfth-grade education

Appendix B

Variable Sources and Descriptions

TABLE B.1. *Variable Sources and Descriptions*

Variable	Source and Definition
Black elected officials	The National Roster of Black Elected Officials reports the total number of black elected officials across levels of government. The natural log is analyzed to correspond roughly to the metric of the other variables.
Jackson 1984	A binary indicator taking the value of one in 1985 and zero otherwise.
Jackson 1988	A binary indicator taking the value of one in 1989 and zero otherwise.
Democratic presidency	A binary indicator taking the value of one under Democratic presidents and zero otherwise.
Income inequality	The GINI coefficient among blacks as reported by the Current Population Survey.
Unemployment rate	The unemployment rate among blacks according to the Economic Report of the President.
Change in inflation rate	The price-deflated change in GDP, Current Population Survey.
Immigration rate	Statistical Yearbook of the Immigration and Naturalization Service.
College enrollment	The rate of college enrollment among high school graduates as reported by the Digest of Education Statistics.
Victimization rate	Serious violent victimization rates by race, created by the Bureau of Justice Statistics using data from the National Crime Victimization Survey and the FBI's Uniform Crime Reports.

TABLE B.2. *Sample Descriptive Statistics*

Variable	N	Mean	Std. Dev.	Minimum	Maximum
Jackson 1984	84	0.0476	0.2142	0	1
Jackson 1988	84	0.0476	0.2142	0	1
Black elected officials	84	8.6050	0.2948	7.8710	9.0070
Victimization rate	84	33.5571	3.3603	25.2000	40.4000
College enrollment	84	44.6691	5.0521	36.5000	55.6000
Income inequality	84	0.4271	0.0255	0.3860	0.4820
Unemployment rate	84	13.8024	2.3561	9.4000	19.5000
Immigration rate	84	2.9667	1.3690	1.8000	7.2000
Democratic presidency	84	0.2619	0.4423	0	1
Inflation rate	84	5.2357	2.5173	2.1000	9.3000
Political work, all	84	0.6202	0.1307	0.3936	0.9728
Political work, male	84	0.3262	0.0706	0.1429	0.4769
Political work, female	84	0.2939	0.0721	0.1663	0.5133
Political work, non-South	84	0.4073	0.1082	0.1635	0.6655
Political work, South	82	0.1993	0.0818	0.0567	0.4368
Organizational work, all	84	0.5282	0.1358	0.3035	0.9092
Organizational work, male	84	0.2627	0.0731	0.1282	0.5234
Organizational work, female	84	0.2655	0.0752	0.1365	0.3936
Organizational work, non-South	84	0.2891	0.0945	0.0678	0.4794
Organizational work, South	82	0.2354	0.0793	0.0881	0.4811
Comp. participation index, all	84	0.6616	0.1395	0.4259	1.0208
Comp. participation index, male	84	0.6834	0.1464	0.3452	1.0654
Comp. participation index, female	84	0.6418	0.1558	0.3863	1.0718
Comp. participation index, non-South	84	0.8070	0.2158	0.3305	1.2571
Comp. participation, South	82	0.4979	0.1709	0.2073	0.9655
Comp. participation, lower status	66	0.2471	0.0777	0.1221	0.4718
Comp. participation, working class	66	0.5755	0.1419	0.3218	0.8896
Comp. participation, middle/upper class	66	1.4162	0.2907	0.8720	2.2949

Appendix C

Time Series Models

Table C.1 presents the findings from three time series models of black civic participation. We use traditional autoregressive moving average (ARMA) models to study movements in black civic participation in the post–civil rights period. Although we use ARMA models instead of intervention models, our ARMA coefficients and statistical tests allow us to determine which set of variables (black empowerment or social and economic distress) are pushing or pulling black civic participation up or down. Like the transfer function weights from a transfer function analysis, our ARMA coefficients provide us with a numerical sense of how much our independent variables influence changes in black civic participation from 1973 to 1994. Our time series tests and model-building procedures follow typical dynamic modeling strategies – descriptive trend analyses, diagnostic checks, and model specification (Cromwell, Labys, and Terraza 1994, 8–10). However, because few scholars use time series models to explain movements in aggregate levels of black civic participation, we will briefly discuss how our substantive arguments can be operationalized using traditional time series analysis techniques.[1]

Before we explicitly modeled movements in aggregate levels of black civic participation over time, we presented a visual plot of each of the

[1] We should note that Danigelis (1978; 1982) used several University of Michigan presidential election year surveys from 1952 to 1976 to examine trends in black civic participation.

TABLE C.1. *Time Series (ARMA) Models of Aggregate Black Civic Participation, 1973–1994*

Independent Variables	Composite Black Participation	Black Political Work	Black Organizational Work
	Coefficients (robust standard errors in parentheses)		
Political Empowerment			
Black elected officials	.27	.08	.12
	(.21)	(.10)	(.10)
Jackson 1984	.04	.02	.01
	(.09)	(.03)	(.05)
Jackson 1988	.05	.04	−.02
	(.07)	(.03)	(.03)
Democratic presidency	−.06	−.02	−.02
	(.05)	(.02)	(.02)
College enrollment	−.01	−.00	−.00
	(.01)	(.00)	(.00)
Economic and Social Distress			
Black income	−.05*	−.02+	−.03*
inequality	(.02)	(.01)	(.01)
Black unemployment	−.01	−.01	−.00
rate	(.01)	(.00)	(.00)
Inflation rate	−.04**	−.02**	−.02*
	(.01)	(.01)	(.01)
Immigration rate	−.04**	−.01	−.02**
	(.01)	(.01)	(.01)
Criminal victimization	.01	.01	.00
	(.01)	(.00)	(.00)
Constant	1.14	.69+	.67
	(.95)	(.41)	(.47)
Wald chi^2 (12)	163.69	3228.86	88.32
Prob. > chi^2	.00	.00	.00
Number of cases	84	84	84

$^{**}p < .01$, $^{*}p < .05$ (two-tailed test), $+p < .10$ (one-tailed test)
Source: Roper Social and Political Trends Data, 1973–1994

black civic participation series in Chapter 3. Next, we investigated whether the participation series were stationary – that is, whether they have a constant mean and variance over time. Our visual analyses indicate that aggregate black civic involvement levels seem to represent a fairly stationary time series because, visually, the mean, variance, and auto covariance of the individual series appear to be time-invariant (Gujarati 1995, 714). The three participation series each exhibit movement and change from 1973 to 1994. In Figures 3.7 and 3.8, we show that aggregate levels of black political and organizational work were generally bound between 0.2 and 0.4 acts, while Figure 3.6 demonstrates that composite black participation levels range between 0.4 and 0.8 civic acts. Furthermore, our statistical tests confirm our intuitions about the general stationary properties of these data.

We examined univariate ARMA model results from the three civic participation series: composite black civic participation, political work activities, and organizational work activities. Next, we conducted augmented Dickey–Fuller (ADF) and Philipps–Perron unit root tests to determine whether the series are I (1) (whether their first difference is stationary).[2] We found that the series are I (1) so we conducted ARMA model analyses of the three participation series. In addition, we conducted normality tests for the series using the normal distribution test. We also graphically examined the aggregate black civic participation series and tested for statistical independence of the quarterly data using Ljung–Box and Box–Pierce tests. Finally, we examined the three series for linear dependence using the Keenan test and the Luukkonen test.

All of these results indicate that a linear-dependence time series model could be reasonably used to examine movements in aggregate levels of black civic participation. Though the method has limitations based on explanations we discuss in Chapter 4, the ARMA approach nevertheless adds perspective to the conclusions we draw from our GLS analysis in Chapter 5. For example, we know from the research literature that the observed aggregate black civic participation level in a given period is partially a function of the overall level of activism in a previous quarter (an autoregressive (AR) element) and a general trend moving average (MA) component. Specifically, in absence of major institutional changes such as the passage of the 1965 Voting Rights Act, similar social forces operating in a prior quarter may largely determine black civic participation levels from one quarter to the next. Furthermore, aggregate black civic participation levels may also reflect a trend or a moving average component, such as the declining rates of

[2] We should note that these unit root tests have low diagnostic power.

civic participation we observed after 1985 (see Table 3.6). Thus, the ARMA model allows us to draw on these two dynamic qualities to explain movements in aggregate levels of black civic engagement since the modern civil rights movement.

Our time series analysis clearly indicates that economic and social distress factors were more important than political empowerment as predictors of movements in black civic participation from 1973 to 1994. Consequently, the results from our ARMA models are consistent with the findings from our GLS analysis. Both models confirm our expectations about how macro-level explanatory factors differentially impact aggregate levels of black civic engagement.

It is important to note that none of the black political empowerment variables in our ARMA models exerted a statistically significant influence on movements in aggregate levels of black civic activism in the period under examination. Neither the presence of black elected officials, the Jackson presidential campaigns, nor college enrollment levels among African Americans affects the movement trend of aggregate black civic participation. This finding is consistent across the composite black participation, the black political work, and the black organizational work models. Thus, black political empowerment forces in these models do not appear to have a long-term effect on movements in aggregate levels of black civic participation.

Most scholarship in black politics highlights the importance of black political empowerment features (such as the number of black elected officials and viable black presidential candidates), but our ARMA models present a different story about the participatory impact of these variables on aggregate levels of black civic participation. These models suggest that black political empowerment variables may exert more of a short-term effect on black participation levels. So, by using ARMA series analysis to examine changes in black civic participation, we see that political empowerment forces (such as the 1984 Jackson campaign) may only serve to mobilize black participation during the campaign period or immediately thereafter, yet diminish or fade away as time passes by and the general political climate returns to its normal course.

Looking beyond black empowerment forces, our analyses also show a consistent pattern regarding the effects of economic and social distress indicators on aggregate-level movements in black civic participation over time. Consistent with our theory of countervailing forces, our three ARMA models show that economic and social distress factors influenced movement trends in black civic activism over time. In particular, as income disparities grew among black Americans, their aggregate levels of civic participation significantly decreased over time. This negative effect occurred for movements in all three types of civic activities. Drawing from our countervailing forces theory, we attribute the robustness of this negative participatory effect to the fact that growing income disparities among black Americans depress the level of group political resources in black communities and lead to lower aggregate levels of civic activism.

Like black income inequality, rising inflation rates also have a consistently negative effect on aggregate-level movements in black civic participation. In periods of increasing inflation, blacks as a group were less likely to engage in civic activities. We suspect that periods of higher inflation adversely affect blacks' participation levels over time by decreasing their income resources, thereby hindering black's ability to participate in civic and political life during tough economic times. The key point of this explanation is that rising price levels limit the economic and material benefits and resources that blacks individually and collectively possess, and thus cause the normal aggregate black participation level to recede in periods of economic hardship.

We also find that the rising rates of immigration to the United States have a fairly consistent negative effect on the movement trend of black civic engagement over time. Rising immigration rates tend to reduce aggregate levels of black civic activism for our composite participation and black organizational work measures. Like the negative effects we find for rising inflation rates, increasing immigration rates appear to erode the wages of black workers in low-skilled and semiskilled occupations. Consequently, at the aggregate level, rising immigration rates decrease the amount of collective economic and material resources from which African Americans can utilize to engage in American civic life.

Finally, our ARMA models show that two of our economic and social distress indicators did not influence movement trends in black civic activism over time. Changes in the black unemployment rate or levels of criminal victimization were not consequential for aggregate-level movements in black civic participation. These results are not surprising given that we found in our GLS models that these variables were not consistent predictors of black participation. Our ARMA models further corroborate our findings from the GLS analysis. These findings confirm part of our speculations about the tug-of-war between black empowerment and social and economic distress. Clearly, the economic forces tug strongly toward pushing black participation downward. However, because our ARMA models do not take into consideration the variations in sample size across quarters, these initial findings must be viewed with caution.

References

Alex-Assensoh, Yvette, and Karin Stanford. 1997. "Gender, Participation, and the Black Urban Underclass." In Cathy J. Cohen, Kathleen B. Jones, and Joan C. Tronto, editors, *Women Transforming Politics*. New York: New York University Press. Pp. 398–411.

Altonji, J., and Card, D. 1991. "The Effects of Immigration on the Labour Market Outcomes of Natives." In John M. Abowd and Richard B. Freeman, editors, *Immigration, Trade, and the Labour Market*. Chicago: University of Chicago Press. Pp. 201–34.

American Political Science Association Task Force Report. 2004. "American Democracy in an Age of Rising Inequality." *Perspectives on Politics*, 4: 651–66.

Arcelus, Francisco, and Allan H. Meltzer. 1975. "The Effect of Aggregate Economic Variables on Congressional Elections." *American Political Science Review*, 69: 1232–9.

Becker, Gary S. 1993. *Human Capital: A Theoretical and Empirical Analysis with Special Reference to Education*, third edition. Chicago: University of Chicago Press.

Bingham, Janet. 1991. "MAD DADS Reclaim Streets." *Denver Post*. October 13, Section C1.

Bobo, Lawrence, and Frank Gilliam. 1990. "Race, Sociopolitical Participation, and Black Empowerment." *American Political Science Review*, 84: 377–93.

Bond, Julian. 1968. *Black Candidates: Southern Campaign Experiences*. Atlanta: Voter Education Project.

Borjas, George J. 1987. "Immigrants, Minorities, and Labor Market Competition." *Industrial and Labor Relations Review*, 40: 382–92.

Borjas, George J. 1998. "The Impact of Immigrants on Employment Opportunities of Natives." In David Jacobson, editor, *The Immigration Reader: America in a Multidisciplinary Perspective*. Malden, Massachusetts: Blackwell Publishers. Pp. 217–30.

Bositis, David A. 1994. *The Congressional Black Caucus in the 103rd Congress*. Washington, D.C.: Joint Center for Political and Economic Studies.

Brown, Elsa Barkley. 1994. "Negotiating and Transforming the Public Sphere: African-American Political Life in the Transition from Slavery to Freedom." *Public Culture*, 7: 107–46.

Browning, Rufus P., Dale Rogers Marshall, and David H. Tabb. 1984. *Protest Is Not Enough: The Struggle of Blacks and Hispanics for Equality in the United States*. Berkeley: University of California Press.

Bunche, Ralph A. 1973. *The Political Status of the Negro in the Age of FDR*. Edited by Dewey W. Grantham. Reprint, Chicago: University of Chicago Press.

Burns, Nancy, Kay Lehman Schlozman, and Sidney Verba. 2001. *The Private Roots of Public Action: Gender, Equality, and Political Participation*. Cambridge, Massachusetts: Harvard University Press.

Button, James W. 1989. *Blacks and Social Change: The Impact of the Civil Rights Movement in Southern Communities*. Princeton, New Jersey: Princeton University Press.

Canon, David T. 1999. *Race, Redistricting, and Representation: The Unintended Consequences of Black-Majority Districts*. Chicago: University of Chicago Press.

Carmichael, Stokely, and Charles V. Hamilton. 1967. *Black Power: The Politics of Liberation in America*. New York: Vintage Books.

Carmichael, Stokely, and Ekwueme Michael Thelwell. 2003. *Ready for Revolution: The Life and Struggles of Stokely Carmichael (Kwame Ture)*. New York: Scribner.

Carmines, Edward G., and James A. Stimson. 1989. *Issue Evolution: Race and the Transformation of American Politics*. Princeton, New Jersey: Princeton University Press.

Carnoy, Martin. 1994. *Faded Dreams: The Politics and Economics of Race in America*. New York: Cambridge University Press.

Cavanagh, Thomas E. 1985. *Inside Black America: The Message of the Black Vote in the 1984 Elections*. Washington, D.C.: Joint Center for Political Studies.

Cavanagh, Thomas E., and Lorn S. Foster. 1984. *Jesse Jackson's Campaign: The Primaries and Caucuses*. Washington, D.C.: Joint Center for Political Studies.

Clark, Kenneth B. 1972. "The Negro Elected Official in the Changing American Scene." In Lenneal J. Henderson, Jr., editor, *Black Political Life in the United States: A Fist as the Pendulum*. San Francisco, California: Chandler Publishing Company. Pp. 150–60.

Cohen, Cathy J., and Michael C. Dawson. 1993. "Neighborhood Poverty and African-American Politics." *American Political Science Review*, 87: 286–302.

Collins, Patricia Hill. 2000. *Black Feminist Thought: Knowledge, Consciousness, and the Politics of Empowerment*, second edition. New York: Routledge Press.

Conway, M. Margaret. 2000. *Political Participation in the United States*, third edition. Washington, D.C.: Congressional Quarterly Press.

Cromwell, Jeff B., Walter C. Labys, and Michel Terraza. 1994. *Univariate Tests for Time Series Models*. Sage University Paper Series on Quantitative Applications in the Social Sciences, 07-099. Thousand Oaks, California: Sage.

Dahl, Robert A. 1971. *Polyarchy: Participation and Opposition*. New Haven, Connecticut: Yale University Press.

Danigelis, Nicholas L. 1978. "Black Political Participation in the United States: Some Recent Evidence." *American Sociological Review*, 43: 756–71.

Danigelis, Nicholas L. 1982. "Race, Class, and Political Involvement in the U.S." *Social Forces*, 61: 532–50.

Dawson, Michael. 1994a. *Behind the Mule: Race and Class in African-American Politics*. Princeton, New Jersey: Princeton University Press.

Dawson, Michael. 1994b. "A Black Counterpublic? Economic Earthquakes, Racial Agenda(s), and Black Politics." *Public Culture*, 7: 195–223.

DeSipio, Louis, and Rodolfo O. de la Garza. 1998. *Making Americans, Remaking America: Immigration and Immigrant Policy*. Boulder, Colorado: Westview Press.

Drake, St. Clair. 1940. *Churches and Voluntary Associations in the Chicago Community*. Chicago: Works Progress Administration.

Drake, St. Clair, and Horace R. Cayton. [1945] 1993. *Black Metropolis: A Study of Negro Life in a Northern City*, revised and enlarged edition. Chicago: University of Chicago Press.

DuBois. W. E. B. [1899] 1996. *The Philadelphia Negro: A Social Study*. Philadelphia: University of Pennsylvania Press.

DuBois, W. E. B. [1903] 2003. *The Souls of Black Folk*. New York: Modern Library.

Dudziak, Mary. 2002. *Cold War Civil Rights: Race and the Image of American Democracy*. Princeton, New Jersey: Princeton University Press.

Dymally, Mervyn. 1971. *The Black Politician: His Struggle for Power*. Belmont, California: Duxbury Press.

Elster, Jon. 1987. *Making Sense of Marx*. New York: Cambridge University Press.

Enders, Walter. 2004. *Applied Econometric Time Series*. Hoboken, New Jersey: John Wiley and Sons.

Erikson, Robert S., Michael B. MacKuen, and James A. Stimson. 2002. *The Macro Polity*. New York: Cambridge University Press.

Farley, Reynolds. 1984. *Blacks and Whites: Narrowing the Gap?* Cambridge, Massachusetts: Harvard University Press.

Fenton, John H., and Kenneth N. Vines. 1957. "Negro Registration in Louisiana." *American Political Science Review*, 51: 704–13.

Foner, Eric. 1988. *Reconstruction: America's Unfinished Revolution, 1863–1977*. New York: Harper and Row.

Foner, Eric. 1993. *Freedom's Lawmakers: A Directory of Black Officeholders during Reconstruction*. New York: Oxford University Press.

Foster, Lorn S. 1990. "Avenues for Black Political Mobilization: The Presidential Campaign of Reverend Jesse Jackson." In Lorenzo Morris, editor, *The Social and Political Implications of the 1984 Jesse Jackson Presidential Campaign*. New York: Praeger Press. Pp. 203–13.

Franklin, John Hope. 1980. *From Slavery to Freedom*. New York: Alfred A. Knopf.

Freeman, Richard B. 1976. *Black Elite: The New Market for Highly Educated Black Americans*. New York: McGraw-Hill Book Company.

Frymer, Paul. 1999. *Uneasy Alliances: Race and Party Competition in America*. Princeton, New Jersey: Princeton University Press.

Fuller, Hoyt. 1975. "Political Motion and the Static Black Condition." *Black World*, 25: 49–88.

Gaines, Kevin. 1996. *Uplifting the Race: Black Leadership, Politics, and Culture in the Twentieth Century*. Chapel Hill: University of North Carolina Press.

Gay, Claudine, and Katherine Tate. 1998. "Doubly Bound: The Impact of Gender and Race on the Politics of Black Women." *Political Psychology*, 19: 169–84.

Giddings, Paula. 1984. *When and Where I Enter: The Impact of Black Women on Race and Sex in America*, first edition. New York: William Morrow and Company.

Gomes, Ralph C., and Linda Faye Williams, editors. 1992. *From Exclusion to Inclusion: The Long Struggle for African-American Political Power*. New York: Greenwood Press.

Goodman, Saul, and Gerald H. Kramer. 1975. "Comment on Arcelus and Meltzer, The Effect of Aggregate Economic Conditions on Congressional Elections." *American Political Science Review*, 69: 1255–65.

Gosnell, Harold F. 1967. *Negro Politicians: The Rise of Negro Politics in Chicago*. Reprint, Chicago: University of Chicago Press.

Guinier, Lani. 1994. *The Tyranny of the Majority: Fundamental Fairness in Representative Democracy*. New York: Free Press.

Gujarati, Damodar N. 1995. *Basic Econometrics*, third edition. New York: McGraw-Hill.

Gurin, Patricia, Shirley Hatchett, and James Jackson. 1989. *Hope and Independence: Blacks' Response to Electoral and Party Politics*. New York: Russell Sage Foundation.

Hamilton, Dona Cooper, and Charles V. Hamilton. 1997. *The Dual Agenda: The African-American Struggle for Civil and Economic Equality*. New York: Columbia University Press.

Harris, Fredrick C. 1999a. *Something Within: Religion in African-American Political Activism*. New York: Oxford University Press.

Harris, Fredrick C. 1999b. "Will the Circle Be Unbroken? The Erosion and Transformation of African-American Civic Life." In Robert K. Fullinwider, editor, *Civil Society, Democracy, and Civic Renewal*. Lanham, Maryland: Rowman and Littlefield Publishers. Pp. 317–38.

Harris, Fredrick C., and Linda F. Williams. 1986. "JCPS/Gallup Poll Reflects Changing Views on Political Issues." *Focus*, 14: 3–6.

Higginbotham, Evelyn Brooks. 1997. "Clubwomen and Electoral Politics in the 1920s." In Ann D. Gordon, editor, *African-American Women and the Vote, 1837–1965*. Amherst: University of Massachusetts Press. Pp. 134–55.

Hochschild, Jennifer. 1995. *Facing up to the American Dream: Race, Class, and the Soul of the Nation*. Princeton, New Jersey: Princeton University Press.

Hochschild, Jennifer L. 1998. "American Racial and Ethnic Politics in the 21st Century: A Cautious Look Ahead." *The Brookings Review*, 2: 43–6.

Iton, Richard. 2000. *Solidarity Blues: Race, Culture, and the American Left*. Chapel Hill: University of North Carolina Press.

Jaynes, Gerald David, and Robin M. Williams, Jr., eds. 1989. *A Common Destiny: Blacks and American Society*. Washington, D.C.: National Academy Press.

Johnson, Cedric. 2004. "The Politics of Race Management: Black Ethnic Politics and American Democracy After Segregation." Paper presented at the Frederick Douglass Institute Works in Progress Seminar, October 2004, University of Rochester, Rochester, New York.

Joint Center for Political Studies. 1987a. *Black Initiative and Governmental Responsibility*. Washington, D.C.: Joint Center for Political Studies.

Joint Center for Political Studies. 1987b. *Black Elected Officials: A National Roster*. Washington, D.C.: Joint Center for Political Studies.

Joint Center for Political Studies. 1988. *Blacks and the 1988 Democratic National Convention*. Washington, D.C.: Joint Center for Political Studies.

Jones, Mack. 1992. "Political Science and the Black Political Experience: Issues in Epistemology and Relevance." *National Political Science Review*, 3: 25–39.

Jordan, Vernon E., Jr. 1980. "Introduction." In *The State of Black America. 1980*. New York: National Urban League. Pp i–xii.

Key, V. O., Jr. 1949. *Southern Politics in State and Nation*. New York: Vintage Books.

King, Desmond. 1995. *Separate and Unequal: Black Americans and the U.S. Federal Government*. New York: Oxford University Press.

Klein, Alec. 2004. "African Americans Getting by, Not Ahead." *The Washington Post*. December 17.

Klinkner, Philip A., and Rogers M. Smith. 1999. *The Unsteady March: The Rise and Decline of Racial Equality in America*. Chicago: University of Chicago Press.

Kousser, Morgan. 1999. *Color Blind Injustice: Minority Voting Rights and the Undoing of the Second Reconstruction*. Chapel Hill: University of North Carolina Press.

Kramer, Gerald H. 1971. "Short-Term Fluctuations in U.S. Voting Behavior, 1896–1964." *American Political Science Review*, 65: 131–43.

Kramer, Gerald H. 1983. "The Ecological Fallacy Revisited: Aggregate versus Individual Level Findings on Economics and Elections, and Sociotropic Voting." *American Political Science Review*, 77: 92–111.

Kryder, Daniel. 2000. *Divided Arsenal: Race and the American State during World War II*. New York: Cambridge University Press.

Ladd, Everett Carll, Jr. 1966. *Negro Political Leadership in the South*. Ithaca, NewYork: Cornell University Press.

Lalonde, R. J., and R. H. Topel. 1991. "Labor Market Adjustments to Increased Immigration." In John M. Abowd and Richard B. Freeman, editors, *Immigration, Trade, and the Labor Market*. Chicago: University of Chicago Press. Pp. 167–99.

Leighley, Jan. 2001. *Strength in Numbers?: The Political Mobilization of Racial and Ethnic Minorities*. Princeton, New Jersey: Princeton University Press.

Lieberman, Robert C. 1998. *Shifting the Color Line: Race and the American Welfare State*. Cambridge, Massachusetts: Harvard University Press.

Logan, Rayford W. 1968. *The Betrayal of the Negro: From Rutherford B. Hayes to Woodrow Wilson*. New York: Collier Books.

Los Angeles Times. 1995. "Central Los Angeles, MAD DADS." September 5, Section 2.

MacKuen, Michael, Robert S. Erikson, and James A. Stimson. 1989. "Macropartisanship." *American Political Science Review*, 83: 1125–42.

Marable, Manning. 2002. *The Great Wells of Democracy: The Meaning of Race in American Life*. New York: Basic Civitas Books.

Markus, Gregory B. 1988. "The Impact of Personal and National Economic Conditions On the Presidential Vote: A Pooled Cross-Sectional Analysis." *American Journal of Political Science*, 32: 137–54.

Marshall, Thurgood. 1987. "The Constitution: A Living Document." *Howard University Law Journal*, 30: 915–25.

Matthews, Donald R., and James W. Prothro. 1966. *Negroes and the New Southern Politics*. New York: Harcourt, Brace, and World.

McAdam, Doug. 1982. *Political Process and the Development of Black Insurgency, 1930–1970*. Chicago: University of Chicago Press.

McClain, Paula, and Joseph Stewart, Jr. 2002. *"Can We All Get Along?" Racial and Ethnic Minorities in American Politics*, third edition. Boulder, Colorado: Westview Press.

Meier, August, and Elliot Rudwick. 1989. "The Origins of Nonviolent Direct Action in Afro-American Protest." In David Garrow, editor, *We Shall Overcome: The Civil Rights Movement in the United States in the 1950s and 1960s*. Brooklyn, New York: Carlson. Pp. 833–930.

Milbrath, Lester W., and M. L. Goel. 1977. *Political Participation*. Chicago: Rand McNally.

Miller, Arthur H., Patricia Gurin, Gerald Gurin, and Oksana Malanchuk. 1981. "Group Consciousness and Political Participation." *American Journal of Political Science*, 25: 494–511.

Moon, Henry Lee. 1948. *Balance of Power: The Negro Vote*. Garden City, New York: Doubleday and Company.

Morris, Aldon D. 1984. *The Origins of the Civil Rights Movement: Black Communities Organizing for Change*. New York: Free Press.

Morrison, Minion K. C. 1987. *Black Political Mobilization: Leadership, Power, and Mass Behavior*. Albany: State University of New York Press.

Muller, T., and Espenshade, T. J. 1985. *The Fourth Wave*. Washington, D.C.: The Urban Institute.

Nelson, William E. 1987. "Cleveland: The Evolution of Black Power Politics." In Michael B. Preston, Lenneal J. Henderson, Jr., and Paul L. Puryear, editors, *The New Black Politics: The Search for Political Power*, second edition. White Plains, New York: Longman. Pp. 172–99.

Nelson, William E., Jr., and Philip J. Meranto. 1977. *Electing Black Mayors: Political Action in the Black Community*. Columbus: Ohio State University Press.

Nie, Norman, Jane Junn, and Kenneth Stehlik-Barry. 1996. *Education and Democratic Citizenship in America*. Chicago: University of Chicago Press.

O'Reilly, Kenneth. 1995. *Nixon's Piano: Presidents and Racial Politics from Washington to Clinton*. New York: The Free Press.

Page, Benjamin I., and Robert Y. Shapiro. 1992. *The Rational Public: Fifty Years of Trends in Americans' Policy Preferences*. Chicago: University of Chicago Press.

Parent, Wayne, and Paul Stekler. 1985. "The Political Implications of Economic Stratification in the Black Community." *The Western Political Quarterly*, 38: 521–38.

Pattillo-McCoy, Mary. 1999. *Black Picket Fences: Privilege and Peril among the Black Middle Class*. Chicago: University of Chicago Press.

Piven, Frances Fox, and Richard A. Cloward. 1979. *Poor People's Movements: Why They Succeed, How They Fail*. New York: Vintage Books.

Preston, Michael B. 1987b. "Introduction." In Michael B. Preston, Lenneal J. Henderson, Jr., and Paul L. Puryear, editors, *The New Black Politics: the Search for Political Power*, second edition. White Plains, New York: Longman. Pp. vii–x.

Price, Hugh Douglas. 1955. "The Negro and Florida Politics, 1944–1954." *The Journal of Politics*, 17: 198–220.

Putnam, Robert D. 2000. *Bowling Alone: The Collapse and Revival of American Community*. New York: Simon and Schuster.

Reed, Adolph, Jr. 1986. *The Jesse Jackson Phenomenon: The Crisis of Purpose in Afro-American Politics*. New Haven, Connecticut: Yale University Press.

Reed, Adolph, Jr. 1999. *Stirrings in the Jug: Black Politics in the Post Segregation Era*. Minneapolis: University of Minnesota Press.

Riley, Russell L. 1999. *The Presidency and the Politics of Racial Inequality*. New York: Columbia University Press.

Robnett, Belinda. 1997. *How Long? How Long?: African-American Women in the Struggle for Civil Rights*. New York: Oxford University Press.

Rosenstone, Steven J., and John Mark Hansen. 1993. *Mobilization, Participation, and Democracy in America*. New York: Macmillan Publishing Company.

Rustin, Bayard. 1971. "From Protest to Politics: The Future of the Civil Rights Movement." In *Down the Line: The Collected Writings of Bayard Rustin*. Chicago: Quadrangle Books. Pp. 111–22.

Schelling, Thomas C. 1978. *Micromotives and Macrobehavior*. New York: W. W. Norton and Company.

Schlozman, Kay L., and Sidney Verba. 1979. *Injury to Insult: Unemployment, Class, and Political Response*. Cambridge, Massachusetts: Harvard University Press.

Shingles, Richard D. 1981. "Black Consciousness and Political Participation: The Missing Link." *American Political Science Review*, 75: 76–91.

Sigelman, Lee, and Susan Welch. 1991. *Black Americans' Views of Racial Inequality: The Dream Deferred*. New York: Cambridge University Press.

Singh, Robert. 1998. *The Congressional Black Caucus: Racial Politics in the U.S. Congress*. Thousand Oaks, California: Sage.

Skocpol, Theda, and Jennifer Lynn Oser. 2004. "Organization Despite Adversity: The Origins and Development of African-American Fraternal Associations." *Social Science History*, 28: 367–437.

Skogan, Wesley G. 1990. *Disorder and Decline: Crime and the Spiral of Decay in American Neighborhoods*. New York: The Free Press.

Smith, Robert C. 1990. "From Insurgency Toward Inclusion: The Jackson Campaigns of 1984 and 1988." In Lorenzo Morris, editor, *The Social and Political Implications of the 1984 Jesse Jackson Presidential Campaign*. New York: Praeger. Pp. 215–30.

Smith, Robert C. 1996. *We Have No Leaders: African-Americans in the Post-Civil Rights Era*. Albany: State University of New York Press.

Stone, Clarence N. 1989. *Regime Politics: Governing Atlanta, 1946–1988*. Lawrence: University Press of Kansas.

Swain, Carol M. 1993. *Black Faces, Black Interests: The Representation of African Americans in Congress*. Cambridge, Massachusetts: Harvard University Press.

Tate, Katherine. 1991. "Black Political Participation in the 1984 and 1988 Presidential Elections." *American Political Science Review*, 85: 1159–76.

Tate, Katherine. 1993. *From Protest to Politics: The New Black Voters in American Elections*. New York: Russell Sage Foundation; Cambridge, Massachusetts: Harvard University Press.

Tate, Katherine. 1994. *From Protest to Politics: The New Black Voters in American Elections*, enlarged edition. Cambridge, Massachusetts: Harvard University Press.

Tate, Katherine. 2004. "Political Incorporation and Critical Transformations of Black Public Opinion." *DuBois Review*, 1 (2): 345–59.

Verba, Sidney, and Norman Nie. 1972. *Participation in America*. New York: Harper and Row.

Verba, Sidney, Kay Lehman Schlozman, and Henry Brady. 1995. *Voice and Equality: Civic Voluntarism in American Politics*. Cambridge, Massachusetts: Harvard University Press.

Walters, Ronald W. 1988. *Black Presidential Politics in America: A Strategic Approach*. Albany: State University of New York Press.

Walton, Hanes, Jr. 1985. *Invisible Politics: Black Political Behavior*. Albany: State University of New York Press.

Walton, Hanes, Jr., and Robert C. Smith. 2000. *American Politics and the African-American Quest for Universal Freedom*. New York: Longman Press.

Weiss, Nancy. 1983. *Farewell to the Party of Lincoln: Black Politics in the Age of FDR*. Princeton, New Jersey: Princeton University Press.

West, Cornel. 2001. *Race Matters*, second edition. New York: Vintage Press.

White, Deborah G. 1999. *Too Heavy a Load: Black Women in Defense of Themselves, 1894–1994*. New York: W. W. Norton.

Williams, Linda F. 1987. "Black Political Progress in the 1980s: the Electoral Arena." In Michael B. Preston, Lenneal J. Henderson, Jr., and Paul L. Puryear, editors, *The New Black Politics: The Search for Political Power*, second edition. White Plains, New York: Longman. Pp. 97–135.

Williams, Linda F. 2003. *Constraint of Race: Legacies of While Skin Privilege in America*. University Park: Pennsylvania State University Press.

Wilson, William J. 1980. *The Declining Significance of Race: Blacks and Changing American Institutions*, revised edition. Chicago: University of Chicago Press.

Wilson, William J. 1987. *The Truly Disadvantaged*. Chicago: University of Chicago Press.

Woodward, C. Vann. [1966] 1974. *The Strange Career of Jim Crow*, third edition. New York: Oxford University Press.

Index